CW01651284

THE REVEREND PRINCE AND HIS ABODE OF LOVE

THE REVEREND PRINCE AND HIS ABODE OF LOVE

Charles Mander

EP Publishing Limited 1976

This edition first published 1976
by EP Publishing Limited
East Ardsley, Wakefield, West
Yorkshire, England

Copyright © Charles Mander 1976

The following have kindly supplied illustrations which we have reproduced in this book: Bath Reference Library; Victoria Art Gallery, City of Bath; The British Museum; County of Dorset County Library; Lambeth Palace Library; St David's University College, Lampeter; National Portrait Gallery; Radio Times Hulton Picture Library; Pigott Collection, Taunton Castle; Mrs Dorothy A. M. Squibbs.

This book is copyright under the Berne Convention. All rights are reserved. Apart from any fair dealing for the purpose of private study, research, criticism or review, as permitted under the Copyright Act 1956, no part of this publication may be reproduced, stored in a retrieval system, or transmitted in any form or by any means, electronic, electrical, chemical, mechanical, optical, photocopying, recording or otherwise, without the prior permission of the copyright owner. Enquiries should be addressed to the Publishers.

ISBN: 0 7158 1198 3

Text set in 11/13 pt. Baskerville

Printed in Great Britain by
Butler & Tanner, Frome and London

Contents

Illustrations

Foreword

The story of Henry James Prince, his association with the Holy Ghost, his gradual transformation into God and his taking the flesh of a virgin to purify the world, has stimulated moralists for many years. The Victorians were shocked by his sexual eccentricities, the Church outraged by his dogmas. The salacious rituals of purification performed in the Abode of Love that he built in Somerset—out of the fortunes of the deluded faithful—have intrigued writers from William Hepworth Dixon to Aldous Huxley.

The clamour of Victorian moralists forced the followers of H. J. Prince to retire behind a barrier of secrecy which lasted well into this century. But in 1957 the contents of the Abode were sold by auction. Mr Ronald Eastwood, the chief County Librarian for Somerset, with great foresight, managed to acquire almost all the literature abandoned by the departing faithful. It is from this treasury of pamphlets and books that I have been able to piece together something of the scandalous history of the Reverend Henry James Prince.

I am much indebted to Mr Eastwood for his constant encouragement and enthusiastic help, both in the original radio programme, and this book. I am also indebted to the many local people who have provided me with material: Mrs Dorothy A. M. Squibbs, widow of the late Philip J. Squibbs, the Bridgwater historian, Mr Lane of the Bridgwater Mercury, Mr Hill of Broomfield who supplied what is, perhaps, the only existing photograph of H. J. Prince, and many other kind people, including an old gentleman of 90 who remembered having two aunts in the Abode.

I dedicate this book to them, to the people of Spaxton, the clients of the Lamb Inn, and the faithful who inhabited the Abode of Love.

The Abode of Love

The village of Spaxton, before the coming of the saints, was little more than a cluster of farm cottages huddled round a public house, the Lamb Inn. The village was located at a crossing of lanes about four miles from the Somerset port of Bridgwater, and about fifteen minutes' walk from the neighbouring parish of Charlinch.

The people of Spaxton, had they wished, need have asked for nothing more—they lived amid some of the finest scenery in the West Country, the great majestic sweep of the Quantock Hills to the west, the Mendips to the north. They could have turned their eyes towards the Elizabethan Rectory and tiny parish church above them on Charlinch Hill. They could, if they had wished. But most of them had been born at Spaxton, would die there, and were not meantime entirely interested in the scenery. The Lamb Inn was a far more attractive proposition.

The village inn served excellent rough cider, known as scrumpy, the wine of the district, at reasonable prices. But the entertainment was limited. After the crops, the weather and the price of fatstock, there was little else to while away the long evenings, except the juice of the apple. At least, that is to say, until the summer of 1846.

The summer of 1846 was a very remarkable one for Spaxton. If the saints did not exactly 'come marching in', as the song has it, they certainly arrived in their landaus and carriages, with grooms and servants. They had come to supervise the building of what was to become the Agapemone, or Abode of Love.

To the customers of the Lamb Inn this was something new,

something unusual; exciting and mysterious as well. Pints of good cider lay abandoned on the bar-top as customers hurried to the roadside to stare in wonder at the strange assembly. The fine ladies and gentlemen had now been joined by an army of workmen, the village was being rapidly transformed.

In the following weeks and months, the Lamb Inn lost much of its regular custom. Even the more dedicated drinkers were lured away from its bar parlour to watch and encourage the sweating labourers who swarmed about the nearby fields. A building was being constructed, a great house with eighteen bedrooms, numerous sitting rooms, dining rooms and servants' halls. Outhouses, stables, conservatories, garden cottages and gazebos were springing up in profusion from more than an acre of Spaxton pasture. Lawns, shrubberies, elaborate flower beds, a postive palace it seems, had arrived mysteriously in the village.

The villagers stood about in perplexed groups discussing the situation, wondering what on earth was going on. The mystery deepened when somebody noticed that the workmen appeared to be building a church. Now why was that? A house, even a palace, people could understand; but a church? What possessed these fine ladies and gentlemen and their fine servants that they should feel compelled to flounder about in the Spaxton mud, supervising the erection of such a strange collection of buildings?

Nobody knew, nobody in Spaxton had the answer. The ladies and gentlemen kept their own counsel and the workmen were as bewildered as the villagers. Then slowly, bafflingly, the buildings disappeared behind a massive brick wall. Only the tall chimneys, the crenellated ramparts, and a ferocious stone lion perched on the roof of the church, its head turned in snarling defiance towards Charlinch Hill, could be seen from the road. The ladies and gentlemen had disappeared as well, their servants with them, lost to view behind the impenetrable brick wall. Reluctantly the people of Spaxton returned to their pints and their cottages. The entertainment, for the time being, was over.

The mystery of the house remained. It was a puzzling, secret place, its doors locked to the outside world. Visitors arrived from time to time—but they were strangers, well dressed, grand looking people from distant places. Nobody from Spaxton, Charlinch, or even Bridgwater could get in, or so it seemed. Tradesmen had to deliver their goods to a disembodied hand that shot out upon the ringing of a bell; it was quite alarming. Not that the tradesmen complained, the hand was well endowed, bills were settled promptly.

Local youths, bolstered by pints of scrumpy and urged on by less intrepid brethren had, on one occasion, attempted to gain entry by climbing the wall. They had returned to the Lamb in considerable disarray, covered in teeth marks, with wild stories about bloodhounds and dripping fangs. The escapade was never repeated, at least not by the locals, who wisely kept their distance. This did not, however, discourage the customers in the Lamb Inn from discussing the subject. Surmise, speculation and endless gossip were enjoyable, rewarding pastimes—providing that the bloodhounds remained behind the walls of the great house.

The villagers were on the whole tolerant. If the fine ladies and gentlemen happened to be lunatics surrounded by mad dogs, that was their concern. Nobody objected to the presence of the strange institution in their midst; in fact on the whole they rather enjoyed it. Conversation had become lively, the weather being hardly even mentioned.

Some of the facts were known already. For instance, the house was called the Agapemone, which is Greek for Abode of Love. The leader of these lunatics, whom they referred to as Beloved, and seemed to worship as a sort of God, was an unfrocked clergyman by the name of H.J. Prince. He was already known in Charlinch; well known. The lion on the roof of the Agapemone snarled towards the parish church with good reason. The husbands of many of the ladies in both villages might have snarled back with equally good reason. For Mr Prince had been curate of the parish church, and Mr Prince had been turbulent, extremely turbulent. Then there was Mr Prince's senior in the living, the once-Reverend Samuel Starky, also unfrocked. He had been Rector of Charlinch for many years, as had his father before him, but he too had been turbulent and had lost his living. Finally there was the once-Reverend George Robinson Thomas, also turbulent, also connected with the parish of Charlinch. It seemed there were quite a number of once-Reverend gentlemen in the Agapemone.

There were women behind the walls as well: gorgeous, expensive, beautiful women, as mysterious as the Agapemone itself. True, one of them happened to be the second Mrs Prince, sister of the once-Reverend Mr Starky, and nothing much to write home about on account of her age and looks. But Mrs Prince was one of many, a hen amongst pullets. The locals discussed the women with interest.

Beloved and his followers emerged from time to time in royal splendour. Travelling in the finest equipage, attended by liveried servants, escorted by outriders, they splashed about the muddy lanes in colourful array.

The small town of Bridgwater is situated on the tidal estuary of the river Parrett. In the middle of the nineteenth century it was a bustling, vigorous seaport. Its cosmopolitan population of merchants, brickworkers, tradesmen and seamen were hard-bitten men of the world, who had been about. The town itself was endowed with an extremely generous proportion of public houses; it still is. Such a population of dedicated drinkers was unlikely to be distracted from its principal occupation during opening time. But even the most dedicated felt obliged to abandon foaming pints of ale and scrumpy to stagger into the street to witness the passing of Beloved and his entourage.

Beloved's expeditions to Bridgwater were preceded by a large man in purple livery who bellowed up and down the high street—'Blessed is he who cometh in the name of the Lord.' The son of God would arrive in splendour, surrounded by a heavenly host of young ladies bound for the dress shops and the welcoming smiles of eager tradesmen. It was a flamboyant gesture, appreciated by everybody.

During the late 1840s and early 1850s the locals were happily entertained by Beloved and his saints and grew fat upon celestial pickings. The inhabitants of the Agapemone were quite obviously mad, they also happened to be extremely wealthy. So if Beloved insisted on being addressed as Lord Prince, and imagining himself to be God, or Napoleon, or Julius Caesar or anything else for that matter, why complain? The tradesmen of Bridgwater and the locals of Spaxton were not fools they were happy to take the money and leave the moralising to others.

Then there was the occasional rumpus, providing exciting diversions to the pleasurable entertainment. One of the younger ladies was kidnapped, carried away by enraged relatives, from under the very walls of the Agapemone. After that episode the bloodhounds arrived in time to foil a second abduction attempt. This time it was one of the inmates trying to remove his wife; he was lucky to escape with his life and one trouser leg.

Some people in the district, mad with excitement, persuaded themselves that Beloved was indeed God and attended open-air meetings to proclaim the arrival of the King of Heaven. The more affluent amongst them actually gained admittance to the Agapemone, disappearing behind

The nearest town to Spaxton was Bridgwater, a bustling river port

When he came to visit the Agapemone in 1867, W. H. Dixon stayed at the Royal Clarence Hotel, Bridgwater, shown to the right of this photograph

the walls forever. Of course there were those who disapproved—parsons and such. Letters were written to the local press, sermons preached about false prophets. But Mr Prince generally gave as good as he got. He was God and that was that; anybody who challenged him was either a fool or a sinner. The more persistent moralists were largely ignored: 'there is no point in casting pearls before swine,' he had written in one of his many pamphlets, 'for they are not worthy of the Kingdom of Heaven.'

But in the spring of 1856 something happened inside the Agapemone that shocked even the tolerant local people and made the moralists shudder. Word leaked out of a ceremony, a strange salacious ceremony, performed in the church before the assembled saints. A virgin had been purified; Mr Prince, disguised as the Holy Ghost, had taken flesh. He had done this in the most obvious way, leaving nothing to the imagination. Moreover he had done it publicly in front of witnesses and in the presence of his wife. He had told the fine ladies and gentlemen that the Lord was amongst them, like a refiner's fire, like fuller's soap, and it was his purpose to extend his love from heaven to earth, from spirit to flesh, from soul to body. A virgin must be found, he had said, suitable to become the bride of the Lamb.

Rumours of Mr Prince's eccentric sexual mores had been circulating the county for some time. People remembered the days of his curacy at Charlinch, how the women had flocked to his prayer meetings. It seemed they had gone in fear and trembling for their souls, weeping, distraught, begging for grace. They had returned in quite a different frame of mind. The manner in which Mr Prince dispensed the grace of God was a secret shared strictly amongst the women. Their menfolk, however, suspected that whatever went on behind the closed doors of the church hall was not entirely spiritual. Their suspicions were in no way pacified by the gleaming eyes and self-satisfied appearance of the returning ladies. If Mr Prince was capable of dispensing that sort of grace as a mere curate, what on earth would he manage as the son of God?

The answer was blindingly revealed by Mr Prince himself in a pamphlet. He had indeed taken flesh. A virgin had been selected and purified, and was even now at his right hand. The flesh had been reconciled to the spirit, a covenant had been made with God, the world was safe from sinners.

Some of the more cynical critics of the Agapemone doubted if it were possible to find a virgin amongst Beloved's followers. They had always suspected that the Abode of Love meant just that—Abode of Love, a sort of private brothel. In this they were quite wrong. There were numerous virgins in the Agapemone and it was far from being a brothel. Beloved had no difficulty in assembling a goodly number of maidens, quivering expectantly in the church that day, and no trouble at all in making his choice. The blushing bride of the Lamb, the flesh selected for reconciliation and taken by the Holy Ghost with the power and authority of God, to the playing of the organ and singing of hymns, was a charming desirable young lady of just sixteen.

The ceremony was known to the faithful as the Great Manifestation. To the world outside it seemed more like rape.

The people of Spaxton, ever vigilant, were naturally the first to notice that all was not well within the Abode. Some of the saints appeared to be escaping, flitting furtively into the night, shaken, pale with shock. This was not altogether surprising. News of the Great Manifestation had rushed like a torrent through Spaxton, Bridgwater, Somerset, to London and the world. Moralists had a field day, society was outraged. The Church rose up in fury, the Press thundered. Less discerning people celebrated the event in less discerning ways. Ribald songs were composed to be sung in public bars, plays were written and broadsheets circulated. It was not surprising that some of the faithful were flitting away.

In the autumn of 1856, nine months after the event, watching customers in the Lamb Inn were intrigued to see saints once more fleeing from the Agapemone. Something else must have happened, something even more soul-shattering than the Great Manifestation. What on earth had the son of God been up to now?

The answer arrived in the form of yet another pamphlet. The sanctified virgin, who could commit no sin, had been accidentally impregnated by the devil. A child had been born, an immaculate conception. The devil, cunning as always, had crept up on the undefiled maiden and put her in the family way. The child was the devil's progeny, and nothing whatever to do with Mr Prince. Not everybody believed in the divine truth of this statement. Outsiders, lacking faith, were inclined to point an accusing finger at Beloved himself. It was, they pointed out, the natural result of the disgusting performance in the church. Beloved was trying to justify his outrageous behaviour by blaming it all, rather unfairly, upon the devil. Once more the Church rose up, once more the Press complained. And saints hurried off into the night.

In the course of time the clamour died down. The doors of the Agapemone remained firmly locked, but whether this was to keep the world out or the saints in, was not clear. It certainly appeared to do both, for the departures quickly became fewer, then stopped altogether. There was nothing left for the customers of the Lamb Inn but to speculate.

Speculate they did—with relish. The good people of Spaxton manufactured all sorts of delicious embellishments to the story of the Great Manifestation.

H.J. Prince became a legend in his time: the Visible Manifestation of God on Earth, the Lord God of Spaxton 'kept a harem in the Agapemone', enjoying a female saint for every day of the week; children were stolen from their mothers' knees by secret agents of the faithful, sent forth to replenish Beloved's seraglio. Terrible orgies of immense proportion and unbelievable promiscuity raged nightly in the Abode of Love; saints who disobeyed, or failed to satisfy Beloved's voracious sexual appetite, were done to death and put away in the garden.

The saints were known to play billiards in the church on Sunday. This was a particularly shocking revelation, far worse than any sex-orgy. The only Sunday game tolerated by Somerset folk was skittles, a good honest game of the people. Billiards was effete, sacrilegious. Customers in the Lamb Inn wrathfully hurled their woods at the ninepins and speculated upon the degenerate kingdom of God in their midst.

But on the whole it was an enjoyable pastime, this endless surmise. Stories of the Agapemone circulated around the county, from pub to pub, generation to generation. They survive today more than a hundred years after the event. It was inevitable that sooner or later some seeker after the truth would wish to visit the Agapemone and record his findings for posterity.

In the autumn of 1867, eleven years after the Great Manifestation, William Hepworth Dixon, a prolific writer and student of the bizarre lunatic fringes of sectarian religion, took a carriage and pair from the Clarence Hotel in Bridgwater and splashed along the muddy lanes towards Spaxton.

Dixon's preoccupation with the bizarre had taken him far afield. 'I have collected my facts in distant places,' he writes in a preface to the fourth edition of *Spiritual Wives*, which contains a biography of H.J. Prince. 'In every case I have seen the people and places for myself.' It is to this searching pioneering spirit that we owe much. For without William Hepworth Dixon the Agapemone, H.J. Prince and the Great Manifestation might well have vanished unrecorded.

It took Dixon eleven years to get round to visiting the Abode of Love, and by that time the furore had died down. The Press had turned to other scandalous matters, such as Roman Catholics and Jews. Nevertheless, the local people, nourished by constant gossip, showed a lively interest in the building and its inhabitants. So much so that the driver of Dixon's carriage was reluctant to proceed any farther than Charlinch Hill. It was not so much the bloodhounds, he informed Dixon, that disturbed him, as the awful thought of meeting people who played billiards on a Sunday. He doubted in any case whether they would be allowed inside. Nobody had gained admittance for years, not even the undertaker. The saints were buried in the garden, sitting up to save space. Nobody visited the Agapemone without an invitation, so why not return to Bridgwater? Or visit the Lamb Inn which was a splendid source of information.

Dixon *had* an invitation. He had written a courteous letter addressed to 'the Lord God, Spaxton, Somerset' and received an equally courteous reply. Admittedly it had not been over-enthusiastic and had not come from the great man himself, but nevertheless it was an invitation. This was a rare privilege. Not many 'sinners' were afforded the honour of a personal interview with the Almighty, and Dixon had been promised just that. Besides, Dixon was intrepid; he had faced arctic winds in the Baltic, circumnavigated the arid prairies of America, he was unperturbed.

Upon reaching the forecourt of the great house, both men were surprised to find that one of the side doors leading to the garden was open. The driver, being no lover of dogs, refused to leave his seat on the carriage top. Dixon, who was made of sterner stuff, descended. He was not rushed upon by snarling bloodhounds, and the man who came in answer to his knocking was not brandishing a billiard cue. The driver, much relieved, hurried off to the Lamb Inn; Dixon, armed with his celestial letter of credit, entered the Kingdom of Heaven.

He was almost certainly the first journalist to set foot inside the Agapemone since the Great Manifestation. He was the first to describe it in any detail, to talk to the faithful and to secure an interview with the son of God. He was a man gifted with a nose for a good story and he also possessed an eye for a pretty woman. He used both to some effect.

The gentleman who emerged from the house was the once-Reverend George Robinson Thomas, Keeper of the Seven Golden Candlesticks, First of the Two Anointed Ones. He was a scholarly, clerical person, who knew how to dress well. That Prince found little difficulty in conning educated, middle-class men and women into accepting such ridiculous titles, condoning his erotic behaviour, worshipping him as God, says as much for his charisma as it does for their gullibility. Dixon, who had spent a great deal of his time poking about amongst deviated christianity, was undoubtedly impressed.

Brother Thomas—for this was the title he used by way of introduction—conducted the journalist to the principal room of the establishment, which turned out to be the church. In spite of his scholarly, well-dressed appearance, Thomas was ill at ease. He seemed unnerved by the presence of the stranger and unwilling to communicate. He was furtive, withdrawn, almost scared. Dixon found this attitude common throughout the Agapemone, except in the presence of Beloved, when the saints seemed to relax a little.

The church was furnished like a Victorian parlour, with easy chairs, settees and antimacassars competing with hassocks, hymn boards and various elaborate ecclesiastical paraphernalia, all surmounted by Prince's own special mystical device: a lion rampant on a bed of roses, supported by a lamb and a dove with the inscription—

ALL HAIL, HOLY LOVE!

Dixon was intrigued to see a billiard table at which the players were women. But the women did not stay; seeing the stranger approaching they dropped their cues in confusion and left. He was now alone with a silent, uneasy brother Thomas.

Dixon had two main reasons for visiting the Agapemone. He sought material for his book—including an interview with Prince—and he had a strong desire to identify the victim of the Great Manifestation. As far as he knew, the girl was still amongst the saints, and would be about twenty-seven. He had discovered that her surname was Paterson, that she had been orphaned as well as raped in the Agapemone, and had subsequently given birth to a child. Beyond that he knew nothing, not even her christian name. To boost the sales of his book he wanted very much to find this girl and to talk to her. He tried pumping Thomas but he was uncommunicative, and the billiards-playing women kept darting in and out with extraordinary frequency. At first he thought this was due to a natural curiosity—strange men not being numerous in the Agapemone. Then he began to feel that there was a purpose, an ulterior motive behind the frequent interruptions. 'I began to see that it was not the habit of this place to allow any brother, any sister, even one of age and rank to hold private conversation with a guest.' The sisters were spying. Thomas could not communicate; he did not dare. This furtive habit of watching and listening was continued remorselessly throughout Dixon's visit.

One of the sisters brought in a tray with a bottle of sherry, a bottle of port and one glass. Thomas, as though on cue, mumbled an excuse and departed. Dixon was left alone. He looked round him at the strange amalgamation of religious and secular furnishing, the bright fire in the hearth, the chimney-piece framed in Gothic oakwork and let in with mirrors. He saw the rich red Persian carpet on the floor, the harp and the organ, the stained-glass windows draped with scarlet curtains, the comfortable red sofa on which he was sitting, and the billiard table. He helped himself to another glass of port, his imagination warmed into activity. This was the room in which the ceremony had taken place, wherein living flesh was said to have been reconciled to God. The atmosphere was thick about him.

A voice floated in through the open window, a child's voice. Dixon crept across the soft red carpet and peered out. A little girl was playing by herself on the lawn outside, a lonely, pathetic, forlorn little figure. Dixon remembered the Final Dispensation. Was this the progeny of the union of flesh and spirit? The room had in it a hush and splendour that affected his imagination.

He turned back to the warmth and comfort of the fire. Prince's mystical device caught his eye—a lion, a lamb and a dove. A virgin must be found, suitable to be the bride of the Lamb. How many virgins had been found for the Lamb? How many times had the flesh been reconciled to God? Would the Lamb be satisfied with just one virgin? The appetite grows by what it feeds on. And what about the lion?

'Will you now come in to see brother Prince?' Thomas was standing by the door.

'Oh yes,' Dixon replied nervously, 'oh yes.' He followed

the Keeper of the Seven Golden Candlesticks as meekly and obediently as any saint.

The room he entered was more like a lady's boudoir than a parlour. There were billowing lace curtains at the windows, chenille coverings and rich delicate furniture. It was a luxurious, seductive, intriguing place with the same euphoric atmosphere Dixon had felt in the church.

Prince, dressed in a black frock coat, a white cravat and shining leather shoes, reclined in divine contemplation amongst his selected acolytes. He was fifty-six years of age at the time, a slight-looking man with a soft, low voice. He had the face of a man not used to being vexed into rage or strife, although in his early years he had thrived on it. His eyes were half closed; he seemed rapt in his own dreams, remote, untouchable, separated from his assembled chosen by his own divinity.

But it was not Prince's divine majesty that riveted Dixon when he entered that room; it was the company he was keeping. The selected few. Two of the saints were men—Samuel Starky, and Thomas, the two anointed ones—the others were women.

All the women present were beautiful, one even 'ravishing'. Dixon was enchanted, such female beauty firing him with inspiration. Seeing his forthcoming book creeping into four, perhaps five editions, he set to work with a will, describing the first lady, sister Annie as 'a very fine model of female beauty; plump, rosy, ripe; with a pair of laughing eyes, a full red cheek, and ripples of curling dark hair.' He is scarcely less enthusiastic about sister Sarah who was young and tall, and sister Ellen who was getting on a bit. But the lady that intrigued him most of all was nestling on the floor beside Prince and gazing adoringly into the master's eyes. She was sister Zoe. 'Sister Zoe was one of those rare feminine creatures who lash poets into song, who drive artists to despair, and cause common mortals to risk their souls for love.'

Was this delectable, lithe young creature, her large blue eyes shining 'with a beaming light', nestling adoringly at Prince's feet, Miss Paterson? Was she the virgin, the unfortunate girl raped so brutally and publicly eleven years ago? Was this the mother of the child in the garden? He wanted to know, he wanted above everything else to know—if only he could get her alone, question her, record her experiences. But first he must be sure.

Prince was prepared to speak at length, to expound his doctrines, to give Dixon a few words of celestial wisdom. The saints talked as well, seemingly released from their bondage by the presence of Beloved, who dropped off to sleep whenever anybody else held the stage.

Dixon listened with polite attention. Although he learned a great deal about the Agapemone, its way of life, philosophy, the history of its occupants, he was never able to penetrate the mystery surrounding sister Zoe. He tried hard enough.

'By what name should I speak to you?' he asked her, during one of Prince's somnolent periods.

'Zoe,' she replied.

'But think,' he urged; 'I am a layman and a stranger; how can I use these sweet familiar names? It would be easier for me to call you Miss——'

'Call me Zoe,' she answered with a patient smile. 'Zoe; nothing but Zoe.'

Later on he tried a different angle.

'Did I not see a child, a little girl, playing on the sward just now?' He was on dangerous ground, but he was determined to winkle out the truth. The reply was really rather nasty. 'She is the broken link in our line of life; a child of shame; a living witness of the last great triumph of the devil in the heart of man.'

'You speak of Miss Paterson's child?'

'She is Satan's offspring—Satan's doing in the flesh.' He must have shivered at that reply which did not come from Prince, who was asleep, but from Thomas, speaking with deep emotion. The atmosphere in the room changed. Dixon could feel the hostility, the emotion, the obsession. They were all affected. All, that is, except for Prince who was asleep, and sister Zoe, 'who kept the sweet serenity of her countenance quite unmoved'. That is the nearest he got to solving the mystery of sister Zoe's part in the Great Manifestation. He had one last try as he was taking his leave.

'May I not hear some word to know you by when I am far away?' he whispered alluringly, taking her hand.

'Yes: Zoe.'

'Zoe . . . what else?' For a moment he saw her lips forming what he thought was going to be the word 'Paterson'. But Prince woke up and answered for her, 'She is Zoe; you must think of her as Zoe; nothing else.'

Dixon has recorded his impressions of the Agapemone in detail and they form the basis for this book. Indeed they must, because such was the secrecy enveloping the place during Prince's lifetime, that nobody else penetrated the bastions of the Abode of Love and returned to write about it. Fragments, of course, exist, speculation galore. It must be said at once that Prince was not altogether deceitful, but freely admitted, even boasted of the Great Manifestation, the ceremony in the church. Just as freely he admitted that he was the visible manifestation of God on earth. And the more furiously the moralists and theologian's denounced him, the easier he found it to equate his persecution with that of

HEPWORTH DIXON.

William Hepworth Dixon, student of the bizarre, whose records of the Agapemone have ensured its immortalisation

Christ. He had an answer for everything, he was unassailable.

When Dixon left the Agapemone, he came away with the distinct impression that Prince was keeping a harem. He was certainly living the life of Riley, enjoying the best of all possible worlds. The lovely young girl who had so impressed Dixon was obviously Miss Paterson, obviously doted on the middle-aged Prince, and was obviously his mistress. The saints lived to serve the man they considered to be God; men and women provided him with every possible luxury. Everything they had went to Prince—the best wines, the finest equipage in the West Country, their wealth, their devotion and possibly their bodies. If he was not God on earth, he came very near to building his own personal paradise in Spaxton.

As Dixon returned to Bridgwater he wondered how it was that so many educated ladies and gentlemen, living in the most conservative society in Europe, if not the world, could be brought to admit the doctrines and breathe the passions of Henry James Prince.

Well may we wonder, too!

Thus the Holy Ghost took flesh in the presence of those whom he had called as flesh. He took this flesh absolutely in his sovereign will, and with the power and authority of God.

'*The Testimony of Brother Prince*'
The Agapemone, *January 1857*

The Maiden Lodger

1811 was a year of destiny. Napoleon was at the gates of Moscow. The British Monarch King George III had finally gone mad. The industrial revolution was producing the Luddite riots and at No. 5 Widcombe Crescent, in the City of Bath, Henry James Prince was born of woman.

History records no sighting of celestial bodies in the eastern sky; wise men were not observed hurrying from distant places bearing gifts. The mad King George, whilst he may have visited Bath, would have been more interested in taking the waters than decapitating the first-born of the municipality, and the Prince Regent was otherwise occupied.

The city of Bath was still a fashionable watering place, the rich and famous jostling with the lame and the halt.

Widcombe Crescent could in no way be compared to Bethlehem, and number five was no stable. The crescent survives today, one of the many beautiful examples of eighteenth-century architecture that makes Bath so attractive to the tourist. Great things were achieved by some of the people who had lived in Widcombe Crescent, who included Henry Fielding the novelist, author of *Tom Jones*. Sir James Brooke, who was building his own paradise in Sarawak at about the time that Prince was building his in Spaxton, has a plaque to his memory at number one. Prince is not so honoured, and the reader can draw his own conclusions.

Henry James was the youngest of seven children, three boys and four girls. He was an ailing child with a disordered stomach, who spent much of his time being sick. His father we know little about, except that he died soon after the arrival of his last born, leaving the family in genteel penury.

Mrs Prince, a sensible, hard-working lady, was left to bring up the large family without benefit of the modern welfare state or a pension; she took in lodgers. The lodgers were neither numerous nor bountiful, but they seemed to have kept the family from the breadline, and one of them was to have some influence on the future Godhead.

The young Prince grew up in a poverty which was not the spectacular deprivation of a street urchin, but the deadening penury of middle-class impecunity. He was a solitary child, frail, precocious, and soon, dreadfully pious. When he was not being sick he was either at church or studying the bible. He informed Dixon that he was perfect in the scriptures by the age of twelve.

Mrs Prince, at the best of times a busy woman, at the worst a desperate one, had enough to do without dancing attendance on her ailing youngest son. She left him largely to his own devices and those of an elderly maiden lodger. This was the lady who was to influence his early life.

Martha Freeman, the daughter of a West Indian planter, had come to Bath on account of her health and advancing age. She was comparatively wealthy, highly impressionable, spinsterish, and a devout Roman Catholic. She became the first, and by no means the last, rich old lady to fall under Prince's spell.

According to Prince, Martha Freeman changed the whole course of his life, bringing him to God, generating his soul to grace. She certainly encouraged his developing piety. She read the Bible with him and prayed loudly, hoping perhaps to capture his soul for Rome; he was Church of England. She also tended his disordered stomach. But change his life she certainly did not—it was her life that was to change.

An extraordinary relationship was built up between the elderly spinster and the precocious child. Martha doted on the boy. His almost perpetual ill-health inflamed her frustrated maternal instinct, his piety her devotion. Prince was not unaware of this. Even as a child he had a powerful attraction for elderly ladies, an ability to play on their emotions, to use them.

Life at No. 5 Widcombe Crescent progressed uneasily. Lodgers came and went, and often there was none at all, except the faithful Martha. Prince spent long hours in his bedroom, closeted with Martha, studying the scriptures and being sick. They read the Song of Solomon together, mouthing the beautiful, sensual phrases.

Behold thou art fair my love; behold, thou art fair; thou hast doves' eyes within thy locks; thy hair is as a flock of goats that appear from mount Gilead.

Martha was captivated. Her ageing body longed for love.

I sleep, but my heart waketh; it is the voice of my beloved that knocketh, saying, Open to me, my sister, my love, my dove, my undefiled; for my head is filled with dew, and my locks with the drops of the night.

It was powerful stuff for the elderly spinster. So powerful that she renounced the Roman faith in favour of the Church of England and fell hopelessly in love. Prince was to use the Song of Solomon with equally devastating effect on many other women.

Mrs Prince, in the midst of her toil, did not fail to notice the flowering of this unhealthy relationship. It was time for her youngest son to leave the nest.

Bath was a haven for the sick and elderly, who thronged the pump rooms in search of the waters of life. They were mostly rich and ready to contribute generously to anybody offering assistance in their losing battle against approaching death. Mrs Prince decided that her son should enter the medical profession. He objected loudly, so did Martha. The boy was pious and perfect in the scriptures. He should enter the Church and take Holy Orders; the world was full of sinners, some of whom the young Prince would bring to God. But Bath was full of rich invalids, and Mrs Prince already had a son in Holy Orders. She was adamant; one parson in the family was enough, she could not possibly afford two. Prince would be apprenticed to an apothecary, moreover it would not be an apothecary in Bath but in Wells some twenty-one miles to the south, well away from Martha. Mrs Prince was a determined woman, so her son was dispatched to Wells. He was sixteen, frail in health and quite unprepared for the rough and tumble of the medical profession.

In 1827 two major organisations regulated the practice of medicine: the College of Physicians, who dealt mostly with university graduates, the forerunners of our present-day consultants, and the Society of Apothecaries.

The apothecaries licensed their members to kill or cure. They were the forerunners of today's general practitioners, and not chemists as is sometimes supposed. Candidates were admitted only after seven years' apprenticeship, and upon the successful completion of a searching examination.

Life for an apprentice was not easy. He was expected to educate himself, especially in Latin, as well as serve his master. During the day he assisted in the various bloodthirsty treatments of the period, including cupping, leeching, blistering and dismembering bodies; during the night he studied, often into the small hours.

For someone of Prince's sheltered background, the life of an apothecary's apprentice must have been traumatic.

Wells, like Bath, was a watering place, though it was not so fashionable, not so crowded. This was an ecclesiastical city, dominated by the great cathedral with its canons, precentors and clergy. A few miles to the south was Glastonbury, the legendary heart of the Christian faith in England. There in the gardens of the ruined abbey was the famous Glastonbury thorn, miraculously sprung from the staff of Joseph of Arimathea, flowering only at Christmas to commemorate the birth of Christ.

The atmosphere, the legends, the mystic symbols of religion may well have been soaked up by the young Prince as he went about the unsavoury business of cupping and leeching. He never neglected his religious education, but attended divine service whenever he could, discoursed earnestly upon spiritual matters with anybody willing to listen, and read the Bible. His medical studies were a different matter.

Medicine was a hit-and-miss affair. An apothecary could sometimes diagnose an illness, he could seldom cure it. He simply did what he could and left the rest to the patient, who more often than not died. Watching his master's ineffectual efforts to delay the inevitable seemed to Prince an unrewarding occupation. The body was corrupt, sinful; disease a punishment from God. But the spirit? . . . that was entirely different. If you could not prevent your patients from hurrying to the hereafter, you could at least help them to get to the right place. If the spirit was healthy, the body would be superfluous. The evangelist was emerging, the Holy Ghost stirring like an embyro in the disordered stomach of the young Prince.

And disordered it had certainly become. The gory business of doctoring, long hours of study, sleepless nights wrestling with the devil, had not improved the young Prince's digestive organs. He fell ill and returned to Bath. Martha was delighted. Armed with the Song of Solomon and a bedpan, she lavished upon her ailing paramour all the comfort and attention at her disposal. Hardly leaving his bedside, she hovered round him like a ministering angel. In the circumstances it was not surprising that the young Prince showed little inclination towards recovery, preferring to

Widcombe Crescent, Bath, birthplace of the visible manifestation of God on Earth. Prince was born at No. 5 and spent his early years there with his widowed mother and brothers and sisters, in a life of genteel penury

languish comfortably in his bedroom at No. 5 Widcombe Crescent.

How much of his condition was psychosomatic is not known. Prince himself informed Dixon in the Agapemone that he was near to death, and that on more than one occasion he received the last sacraments in the presence of Martha. This may be true, on the other hand it may not. Prince was quite capable of enjoying ill-health, capable of simulating a disordered stomach to achieve his own ends. He was a determined young man who much preferred the comfort of his bedroom and the attentions of Martha to the grinding toil of doctoring in Wells. There is no doubt the symptoms existed and tormented him for many years, but they could have been largely self-imposed.

There is also no doubt that Mrs Prince was unimpressed by the gravity of her son's illness. She was a practical woman, had few illusions about him and disapproved of his unhealthy relationship with Martha. She was just as determined as her offspring, determined that he should follow a medical career without the distracting attentions of her principal lodger. Since Martha was her one constant guest—at times her only source of income—it would be madness to send her packing. Better to lose a son. Consequently, whenever the opportunity occurred, she flushed the pale, protesting youth from his bedroom and returned him to Wells. Prince, equally determined, popped back to Bath like a yo-yo.

The battle of wills raged for almost five years. Eventually Mrs Prince lost patience. Her son's apprenticeship was in shambles; he seemed to spend more time on the road between the two cities than cupping and leeching. Martha was a menace, perpetually flying to his bedside, encouraging his ever-frequent vapours when he was at home, and weeping for him when he was away.

If the young Prince was to become a doctor he would have

to be driven out of the county, out of reach of Martha. Acting upon the advice of Prince's employer—no doubt gratefully received—she sent the young man to London. He was to go to Guy's Hospital and the Webb Street Medical School for cramming. Prince departed under protest. It was probably the first and only time he was to be defeated by a woman.

Guy's in 1831 was not the efficient establishment it is today. It was more like a madhouse. The staff were self-assertive and quarrelsome, the patients filthy and neglected, the students given to boozing and brawling whenever they had the money to do so.

Coming upon this imbroglio fresh from his bedroom in Bath, Prince must have thought that he was entering the kingdom of the damned. The corridors were crammed with squabbling physicians, slatternly nurses and brawling students. Blood-soaked surgeons brandishing severed limbs, the screams of demented patients, and the groans of the dying, did little to encourage him in his unchosen career.

Strangely enough he survived. He attended Mr Guy's hospital for nearly two years and there is not one mention of a stomach disorder. The work was backbreaking. Lectures were followed by ward duties, then by long hours in the post-mortem and dissecting rooms amongst rotting corpses, with even longer hours studying by candlelight in a rat-infested back room in the Borough. There was no time to think about stomach disorders, no time to think about anything except work and keeping alive.

Prince went about his studies in a pious cocoon, insulated from the horrid world of Guy's, contemplating damnation, equating disease with the sins of the flesh. His behaviour was impeccable. One of Dixon's fellow-students, a Dr Noble, describes him as living like a saint—'neither drinking, swearing, gambling or running wild in love, pure in thought, clean in fact, offended by vice not only in feeling, but in taste.' Rare qualities amongst medical students!

In 1832 he passed his final examinations and was admitted to the Society of Apothecaries. He was now a doctor of medicine. Prince returned to Bath and promptly fell sick; Martha hurried to comfort him.

The following two years were divided between the pleasurable comfort of languishing in Martha's arms and the less pleasurable occupations of doctoring in the Bath General Hospital. It was about this time that Prince started keeping a journal, and from the morass of theological megalomania we begin to get a misty picture of a growing evangelical intensity. As a doctor his bedside manner was startling. He seemed more intent on reducing his patients to gibbering mental wrecks over the state of their souls than curing their bodies. Here is an example, the victim in this case being a Mrs Cooper who is on her death bed. She seems to have been cheerful enough until Dr Prince arrived.

'I frequently visited her, and spoke to her most solemnly of her awful state, which I put before her in the most appalling picture of death and eternal damnation.' The good lady replied that she was very happy, and prayed to God to take her out of her misery. Prince was not impressed; as the illness continued he observed that Mrs Cooper appeared to become more wicked and to yield to the most 'horrid passions'. These horrid passions were directed at the lady's husband who, for some reason, irritated her. 'She would damn her husband to hell and swear she would tear the eyes out of his head, if she could get out of her bed; but the palsy of her legs prevented her.' Which was probably just as well for Prince as it was for her husband. The journal continues—'About three weeks ago, when passing her door, I went to see her. I used to have a strange sensation of dread when I went into her chamber, as if I realised the presence of Satan about her bed, waiting for his prey; so that I ever went in prayer and dependance upon Christ. On this occasion I was just about tc leave her in despair, when I thought she seemed to take a little more interest in what I said, when explaining the reason that she did not fear death; viz. her own blindness.'

Sensing victory, he pressed on, tormenting the wretched woman with visions of hell and damnation. A few days later he announces triumphantly in his journal—'The truth appeared to have flashed upon her suddenly, and was accompanied with such conviction and terror, that she quite trembled in bed from fear: to use her own words, "she had the horrors". What a wonder-making God! How full of faithfulness and love! "Worthy is the lamb that was slain". Amen.'

The journal is crammed with similar accounts of pyrrhic victories and raging battles with the souls of patients. It seems that nobody in Bath General Hospital could die peacefully. They must have dreaded the presence of the pious young doctor looming over them like an avenging angel. No expiring sinner would be allowed to shuffle off his mortal coil with tranquillity as long as Prince was around. Death was sin, the process of dying utterly sinful; nobody escaped.

Neither, to do him justice, did he spare himself. Not a day passes in his journal without an account of some phrenetic encounter with the devil in his own flesh. Corruption was everywhere, the sins of the flesh constantly battled with the spirit in the body of H.J. Prince. He was immensely attractive to women and obviously attracted by them. His naturally strong sexual desires had to be subjugated and lascivious night thoughts driven away. Lust for the pleasings of a pretty woman, the temptations of a naked thigh, plump buttocks and firm beckoning breasts were the work of the devil. He was locked in combat with that formidable spirit, night after night. He denied the devil his due by concentrating on the bleeding body of Christ on the cross, channelling his sexual longings into spiritual longings. Sometimes his feeling of guilt was so intense, his sexual desires so strong that he was physically affected: 'Under these terrors of the Lord I lost sight of Christ entirely; my agony became extreme; I could not utter a word of prayer; I really believed myself to be going down into hell. My horror increased to such an extent that I was on the verge of fainting; and when I was able to rise, my body trembled and perspired so fearfully I thought I must have rung for assistance.'

It is interesting to note that the vast majority of Prince's spiritual castigations were applied to women. He lashed their souls with a kind of violent relish, used them indiscriminately for his own ends, until finally he raped one in the church of the Agapemone. Had he not been forced by his own sense of morality and the morality of the age to suppress his strong natural desires from the very first, there might never have been an Agapemone.

Prince's relationship with Martha was never overtly sexual. She was not an attractive woman, being elderly and frail, thoroughly pious and probably rather tiresome. But she doted on him, tended him with loving care and obeyed him slavishly. In return he accepted her devotion, allowed her to lavish her wasted love and affection upon him, and occasionally encouraged her to believe that it was mutual. She did not attract him sexually but she was convenient, useful. He was undoubtedly fond of her in his own way, but never as fond of her as she was of him, and he was of God, which meant himself.

In 1834 Prince was in some measure to get a taste of his own medicine. His toil in the hospital, coupled with long hours wrestling with the devil, increased his stomach disorder and he was forced to ride to London to consult a specialist.

We do not know the nature of his illness; a disordered stomach could mean almost anything. Prince obviously did not know and it seems unlikely that the specialist knew. But being curious he decided to operate. The unfortunate Prince nearly bled to death.

The operation was performed without anaesthetic, and along with its consequences it changed the course of Prince's career. During the five weeks the unhappy patient was confined to his room he was visited by a series of apocalyptical dreams. Martha, adorned in white raiment, mystic and wonderful, floated dreamlike before his eyes, urging him to higher work. She seems to have had rather more influence over him in this form than in life, for he felt inspired on the 7th of May 1834 to make the following declaration in his journal: 'In the afternoon, at half-past four, having suffered under conviction of sin fifteen months, and during the last month with the utmost agony, it pleased God, of his infinite mercy, to reveal His Son Jesus Christ to me, by faith whilst I was in earnest prayer in my bedroom. May my life, body and soul, be devoted wholly to the service of Him who died for me, from this time forth for evermore. Henry James Prince.'

He was twenty-four. The future Messiah was emerging.

The Son of Man so loved the earth that He gave his own Spirit, that whosoever believeth in Him should not die, but be alive, and abide the coming of the Lord,
BEHOLD HE COMETH!

Brother Prince
The Agapemone, August 15th, 1856

Folly and Depravity

Prince had decided to devote his life, body and soul wholly to the service of God. Ailing humanity would have to struggle on without him. He abandoned the medical profession, resigned his post at the hospital and retired to Widcombe Crescent to pray with Martha. Mrs Prince was not overjoyed.

The emerging Messiah showed no desire to work for a living, neither did he emerge. On the contrary, he became an expensive recluse. He spent hours locked in his bedroom with Martha, pondering over the Song of Solomon and, for all Mrs Prince knew, other things as well! Once again something had to be done, once again it was her son who was sent packing.

The operation on Prince's stomach, in spite of divine intervention, had merely enriched the surgeon. The disorder remained. Mrs Prince, ever resourceful, recruited local medical opinion to urge her son into taking a long convalescent holiday. Travelling, they all agreed, would do him good. Sea breezes and the bracing climate of Scotland would be excellent tonics. Bath was no good for disordered stomachs; if he stayed he would probably decline, possibly die. In the face of such powerful arguments and ever-increasing indigestion, Prince succumbed. He would take a cut-rate grand tour of the British Isles, visiting friends and relations on the way. Mrs Prince was relieved because the journey would keep him occupied and away from home; it might even bring him to his senses. She was right in her first two assumptions, predictably wrong in her last. Nothing would bring Prince to his senses, not even the Holy Ghost.

It seems unlikely that Mrs Prince could have financed the journey. She may have scraped some of the money together; she was sufficiently desperate. Prince was above troubling himself over such mundane matters. The Lord would provide for him, which at this time generally meant Martha. So it was probably Martha who supplied the cash. She may not have wanted to. The prospect of being separated from her soul-mate for such a long period could not have been very attractive. But she was his slave, entirely devoted, utterly obedient.

Martha was never at her best outside the context of No. 5 Widcombe Crescent. There she fulfilled her role as a ministering angel, constantly attending the increasing demands of her divine sweetheart. Away from home she felt insecure and tended to fall sick. This was something that Prince discovered in later years and found tiresome. She would not, in any case, have been encouraged to go with him; it would not have been proper and it would have defeated Mrs Prince's well-considered plans. Prince, himself, was probably indifferent, he used Martha as he used all women. Moreover, he had laid his own plans and these required Martha to remain at home, close to his mother. So she did not travel with him, at least not in body. Her spirit, of course, would be his constant companion; but that did not worry Mrs Prince.

H.J. Prince's account of his travels is a mixture of developing outrage at the advancing tide of depravity and an equally developing sanctimonious self-righteousness.

On the 30th of July 1835 he sailed on board the cutter *Wyvern* from Bristol to the Channel Islands. The little boat tossed uncomfortably on the choppy waters of the Bristol Channel, and Prince was encouraged to commit himself to God and retire to his cabin. The cabin was more of a closet, a partition in the foredeck, where he passed an uneasy night on a shelf with a blanket and counterpane, but no sheets.

The choppy weather did not affect his fellow passengers, three gentlemen—part of the advancing tide of depravity—who sat into the small hours drinking, smoking and swearing generously. Prince, huddled on his shelf, could not find the energy to reprove them.

On the 3rd of August the *Wyvern* docked at St Peter Port, Guernsey, to discharge part of her cargo before continuing to her ultimate destination, the island of Jersey.

Prince put up at a boarding house in New Town during the three days the ship was in port. His stomach, as always, was disordered and he was tormented by toothache. But this did not prevent him from getting about, neither did it discourage him from observing the sinful behaviour of those around him. 'The conversation was such as my soul abhorreth—unholy. I begin to discover out of what a horrid pit I have been drawn by the rich grace of God.' That Prince should have been so shocked by mundane small talk in a Guernsey boarding house is surprising. He must have heard much worse at Guy's. It may have been toothache, or a sense of middle-class morality that outraged him on this occasion. He was certainly far less displeased the following day when he visited a kind of Bridewell on the other side of the island. 'The arrangements are very good, it is rather a poor-house, with a house of correction and dispensary—solitary confinement employed; Magdalens admitted as such, but afterwards return to their old courses.'

The Channel Island prostitutes were spared castigation, perhaps they were beyond redemption. The establishment as a whole was inspected eagerly with a speculative eye. 'Two hundred and fifty inmates, among them some deranged; a boys' and girls' school attached; all very neat; most likely to be useful in affording opportunity for spiritual instruction.' Fortunately for the inmates, especially the boys and girls, Prince had only three days in Guernsey. Some years later he was to 'afford spiritual instruction' to a Sunday school in Somerset with disturbing results.

The *Wyvern* sailed for Jersey. During the short voyage Prince set about one of the blaspheming passengers, a tentative experiment in bringing a sinner to God. The exercise was a dismal failure. The subject, who showed not the least desire for repentance, aggressively directed the evangelist to take his services elsewhere. Prince retired to his closet and wrote in his journal: 'Fear of man is infinitely stronger in me than love of man.' He was beginning to discover that a large aggressive male sinner was a more daunting prospect for the Holy Ghost than a dying old woman. But he was not unduly discouraged, the spirit would return to the fray.

Jersey, like Guernsey, was full of folly and depravity. There were bucolic colonels swearing in boarding houses, trifling small talk, sinful blasphemy. 'I cannot hold fellowship with these people, they contrive to interrupt my communion with my saviour.' It was a parlous state of affairs, and on top of it all there was the toothache, not to mention the disordered stomach. Prince left the island on the next steam boat for Southampton, nursing his tooth and his stomach amidst the cursing of passengers in the fore cabin.

At Southampton he seems to have recovered, both in health and spirit. There are no mention of toothache or intestines. But there is a great deal of spiritual comfort, particularly amongst the ruins of Netley Abbey, which pleased him greatly.

He was not quite so pleased to find a letter from his mother awaiting him at the post office at Portsmouth.

For some time now Prince had been moved by the Holy Ghost towards taking orders in the Church of England. Perhaps he felt in need of assistance, the spirit was not completely upon him. Once it was, of course, he would throw the Church aside; in the meantime he would need to use it.

Soon after his departure from Bristol he had written a long passionate letter to his mother, demanding her acquiescence and financial support. Her reply awaited him at Portsmouth; it gave him no pleasure. Mrs Prince was predictably against any such idea, her letter was almost vehement. Prince prayed for her soul and wrote to Martha. He would use her as an ally to wear down his mother; he had not left her behind for nothing.

Mrs Prince resisted stoutly. She had gone to considerable trouble and expense to turn her son into a doctor and could see no reason why she should be put to further trouble and expense to turn him into a parson. She could hardly be blamed for this. Her son may have considered himself the Messiah, but she was no Virgin Mary, just a harassed housewife with doubts about her son's sanity. No. 5 Widcombe Crescent resounded to genteel bickering as the two women battled for the future of the young man.

Prince passed on to London; the Lord would guide him, He would decide. Prince was beginning to establish a tentative 'direct line' to the Almighty for divine orders. The Almighty, as usual in these matters, worked in mysterious ways.

During his stay in London he had some doubts as to the wisdom of buying 'pamphlets and tracts for distribution'. He laid the matter before the Lord in prayer, who sent him an answer in the person of a certain Mrs W., who appears to have been a divine messenger. 'She recommended me to do both, almost without asking her,' he records in his journal, 'commit thy way unto the Lord, trust also in him, and He will bring it to pass.' Ordinary mortals might very well hesitate to bother the Deity over such a small matter. But Prince was no ordinary mortal.

The wisdom of divine guidance wore a bit thin at times. The Holy Ghost was moved to distribute the tracts and pamphlets to the crew of the ship en route from London to Scotland—a rash, impulsive gesture. Seamen are well used to missionary zealots and have ways of dealing with them. Prince does not record their reactions in his journal, but it was probably unprintable!

He arrived at Edinburgh on the 27th of August, where he spent the best part of six weeks accepting lavish hospitality from friends and scourging their souls in return. In the circumstances it is a wonder that Prince had any friends at all. He disapproved of almost everything and everybody, stalking through life in a state of outraged purity, laying about friend and foe alike. But he never lacked admirers, was never short of hospitality and was seldom crossed. His attraction for women was enormous. Without exception they adored him. He was not tall, neither was he handsome; it was his personality that captured them.

Aldous Huxley in his essay, 'Justifications', describes Prince as a snake-charmer, a lion-tamer, who could dominate his fellow-men and women without effort. He could certainly dominate women, treating them like inferior beings, lashing them with his tongue as they worshipped at his feet. The more he castigated, the more they worshipped. The more callously he used them, the better they enjoyed it. There was a good deal more to Henry James Prince than the odour of sanctity.

On the 14th of October he went south to visit his brother. The visit was decisive, momentous.

John Prince was Rector of the parish of Shincliffe, a small improverished village about five miles from the city of Durham. He was also one of the many reasons for Mrs Prince's objections to her youngest son's religious aspirations. Shincliffe was a destitute, brawling, brutal little village. The parish provided a threadbare living for the incumbent. The church, a converted barn, was rarely patronised, the congregation a mere handful of old ladies. The locals beat their wives, cherished their dogs, and boozed whenever they had the time and money. The gentry, such as they were, preferred sporting activities on a Sunday to attending divine service. It was probably no different from a thousand other parishes at the time.

Prince was outraged. He observed his brother's exhausted ministry with disdain. If this was the Church of England in action, then God help the righteous. The bastions were tottering, and the devil rampant in Shincliffe might well be rampant elsewhere. Prince decided beyond doubt that the established Church in England was in desperate need of his services. He hurried back to Bath.

On the journey it must be recorded that the Holy Ghost was soundly trounced by an eleven-year-old schoolboy, probably the only admitted defeat of that deity in battle. It happened in the coach between Birmingham and Worcester: 'Had for my companion part of the way a very shrewd and well-informed boy, eleven years old, who argued stoutly for infidelity, doubted the truth of the Bible, and the existence of heaven; he went to the horrible extreme of taxing our Saviour with theft, in having stolen a colt, the foal of an ass. After replying to all his objections, I warned him of his awful condition and besought him to repent; he sneered and composed himself to sleep.' Prince, rocked back on his heels by the devilish cunning of his opponent, could only mutter darkly in journal—'what a striking example of human depravity'.

Back at Widcombe Crescent, once more in the loving care of Martha Freeman, Prince prepared himself for battle. His mother was still violently opposed to his entering the ministry. Martha, never the most assertive of women, had done little more than irritate Mrs Prince with her efforts on his behalf. Prince was made of sterner stuff, and God was on his side.

He did not bother to argue with his mother; his very presence at Widcombe Crescent was enough to drive her to distraction. He returned to his usual pastime of castigating ailing humanity. This now had nothing to do with medicine and was, therefore, unpaid. He also retired to his bedroom with his beloved Martha to study for the ministry.

These unprofitable occupations wore down his mother's resistance, so that when he was moving for a period towards revivalism, collecting the neighbourhood women into a wailing prayer group in his bedroom, Mrs Prince went to pieces. The lodgers were complaining about the noise, and some of them were leaving. She wildly suggested Oxford as a suitable establishment for her son's theological studies. It may have been the first thing that entered her head in her distraction; it was certainly impractical and far too expensive. Prince, hardly magnanimous in victory, berated her for lack of humility, accusing her of being a snob. Even Martha could not afford Oxford. And Martha was going to have to pay—she was happy to do so. Martha would do anything her beloved wished and more.

In the end they settled for St David's College, Lampeter, in North Wales. The local Vicar, a Mr B., was acquainted with the Vice-Principal and felt sure that he would find a place for the young man to oblige an old friend. Lampeter was cheap and conveniently far from Bath; it was not Oxford or Cambridge but it would do. Mrs Prince agreed—she was ready to agree to anything by now. Mr B. wrote to his friend the Vice-Principal who obligingly offered to take the young man under his wing, and lived to regret it. Mr B. had done his friend a startling disservice.

The Reverend Alfred Ollivant, Vice-Principal of St

David's College, Lampeter, was a man of the world. He bore a remarkable resemblance to the Duke of Wellington, which set him apart from ordinary mortals. Like the Duke, he was ambitious, fond of riding to hounds and knew the difference between port wine and claret. His intellectual qualifications were impeccable. He was a senior medallist and a high wrangler of Cambridge University, brilliant in his craft, a master of the subtleties of verbal fencing. He was destined in the course of years to become Bishop of Llandaff; in the meantime he kept a sharp eye on anything that might help him on his way. Like many emerging prelates of the day, he was less concerned for the souls of sinners than his own advancement in the Church. Accepting Prince as a divinity student was one of his less distinguished achievements, but he was not to know this. The blame must lie squarely upon the shoulders of the Reverend Mr B., who had some idea of Prince's disruptive qualities, Mrs Prince, who knew her son all too well, and the besotted Martha.

Since Martha was going to foot the bill, Prince felt it wise to pay her a little more attention than usual. She was deeply in love with him, as she had been for many years. But if he was to survive at Lampeter without starving, it was vital to make sure that her devotion was absolute. He cultivated her assiduously, wooing her with the Song of Solomon, seducing her with spiritual cupidity.

This curious method of courtship, this erotic mixture of sanctity and sex, was one of Prince's principal weapons. He used it on any number of victims. Sister Ellen, speaking to Dixon in the Agapemone says, 'You must not think of Brother Prince as courting and marrying in the usual way; both his wives have been older than himself; Martha was an old woman when he took her.' The Song of Solomon is easily misconstrued, it is capable of conjuring up all sorts of salacious images. Martha was his Beloved, his rose of Sharon,

St David's, Lampeter. It was here that Prince started a fanatical prayer group known as the Lampeter Brethren. Having disrupted the St David's establishment many of them were later to become founder members of the Abode of Love

fairest among women; honey and milk were under her tongue; her breasts like two young roes. He was her Solomon, comely as Jerusalem, terrible as an army with banners; her bowels moved for him. It was powerful seductive imagery and Prince knew it. He led her on, tempting, tantalising, playing her like a hooked fish, arousing sleeping passions until she trembled with desire, burned with unrequited love. He probably never favoured her—copulation was the work of the devil, a sin of the flesh. This was a spiritual affair, divine, holy, of the soul. He was playing his cards with skill, binding the besotted old lady to him. 'She is not the supreme object of my affections, nor occupies the place of an idol in my heart,' he wrote in his Journal on their wedding day—hardly the words of a committed lover. But the wedding day was in the future, Prince was not ready to marry Martha just yet. He had all he needed for the time being: a place at Lampeter, a generous allowance to keep him comfortable during his studies, and a famous victory over his mother.

He retired to his bedroom, to rejoice in the Lord and prepare himself for his new vocation as a divinity student. The Reverend Alfred Ollivant sipped his port wine in the tranquillity of his apartments at Lampeter, blissfully unaware that the son of God was about to burst upon him.

Poor, poor, fallen man! so deeply sunk in ignorance and sin, so far gone in folly and depravity; I do weep for thee, I do pray for thee! Alas!

Brother Prince. 'Journal'
August 9th, 1835

The Lampeter Brethren

St David's College, Lampeter, was a new foundation. It had been created to serve as a bastion of conformity in a sea of dissent. Nonconformism in its various forms had all but overwhelmed the Established Church in Wales. From the mining villages and valleys of the Rhondda, it had spread northwards, threatening the hitherto comfortable dominion of the Welsh clergy. Chapels and meeting houses with formidable names and served by wild-eyed evangelists of dissent sprang up throughout the land.

Damnation, as preached from chapel pulpits, fascinated the people of Wales with its dramatic intensity, as much as it terrified the bishops and clergy of the Anglican establishment.

Lampeter had been built quickly in an attempt to stem the tide. It provided theological training on easier terms than Oxford, Cambridge or any other college similarly endowed. Its graduates, mainly Welsh, were intended to be flung into battle. They would go forth as champions of orthodoxy, warriors of conformity. Thoroughly trained in the arts of theological disputation with a sound knowledge of the scriptures, the graduates of Lampeter College would issue forth to win back the mining villages to the true Church. To this end it had been constructed, but to this end it was not entirely successful.

The college was situated amongst some of the most beautiful scenery in the whole of Wales. Many of its students had been seduced from the path of duty by the abundance of trout streams in the vicinity, many more by the abundance of good Welsh beer flowing in village taverns. They had become worldly, preferring field sports to divine worship, quoting Horace rather than the scriptures. This was only too apparent to the son of God as he arrived to take up residence on the 8th of March 1836. He was outraged!

'This place is truly a land "not sown",' he remarks with some feeling in his Journal; 'the very forms and ordinances are scorned by those about to enter the ministry. One might think they were educating for the stage rather than the pulpit. My soul wearies of the filthiness of Horace.'

Compared with the average student, Prince was elderly, approaching twenty-six. The green salad days, if they had ever existed, were over. Life was serious, sinners rampant everywhere. He regarded the jolly students of Lampeter with a beady eye and consulted the Holy Ghost.

Prince was by now consulting the Holy Ghost frequently, seeking divine guidance in all matters. For instance, if he wished to cross the road and it was raining, he would not unfurl his umbrella without prior 'consultation'. This often gave strangers the impression that he was talking to himself. Some of the directives he received from above were so impulsive and eccentric that some of his associates were driven to the conclusion that he was unhinged. They may have been right, for, in his own words, he was, 'passing through life' and coming out on the 'other side of God'. The process was bound to be alarming to the layman. But Prince was not all that mad. His working relationship with the Holy Ghost was a profitable one, the spirit having a fair measure of business acumen.

The jolly students of Lampeter, together with the Vice-Principal, would soon feel the weight of H.J. Prince and the Holy Ghost. The college had strayed from the line of duty, and would be returned to the rails. The Vice-Principal and his effete establishment would tremble at the wrath of God.

Prince set about collecting a group of like-minded fellow students. Not everybody at Lampeter had succumbed to Bacchus, neither were they all callow youths. One of the first to fall under Prince's influence was Arthur Augustus Rees. In some ways Rees had much in common with Henry Prince. They were both mature students, both qualified in other professions. Rees had served in the Royal Navy as a midshipman in H.M.S. *Britannia*, a 120-gun ship of the line. On the face of it, this was an unlikely background for an emerging clergyman, but the sea is a powerful element, and seamen struck by a sense of their own inadequacy in the face of nature occasionally turn to God. Rees was such a one; so, in later years, was Prince's successor at the Agapemone.

The two young men struck up an immediate friendship. They occupied adjacent rooms in the college lodgings, were both serious-minded, pious and prayerful. Prince, as always, was the dominant partner—he never came second to anybody during the whole of his life. But Rees was no doormat; in the course of time he saw through Prince and became his principal and most outspoken opponent. But at Lampeter they were firm friends, Rees admiring his zealous comrade to the point of worship. 'I did never see or hear an individual more thoroughly devoted to God,' Rees wrote of his friend. 'From the day of his matriculation to that on which he quitted college, he was the glory of the institution, both in scholarship and piety; from first to last he exhibited such a steady, consistent and well-regulated course of conduct, as commanded the approbation of his tutors, and the respect of his fellow students.'

This may have been Rees's opinion of Prince; others, such as the Reverend Alfred Ollivant, considered him to be a confounded nuisance. Prince had taken an immediate dislike to the Vice-Principal, considering him an image of clay, a wolf in sheep's clothing, a creature on which the devil had set his mark. Ollivant was everything that Prince subconsciously wanted to be: a free-living clerical gentleman with influence and power in the Church. Prince resented his easy superiority, his brilliant wit, his likeness to the Duke of Wellington. To him it was the mark of the devil. He ground his teeth and set out to embarrass the Vice-Principal in any way he could.

Together with Rees he formed a prayer group of intense young zealots gleaned from the more earnest students at the college. They gathered together, like the women at Widcombe Crescent, to pray loudly for the souls of perishing sinners. They prayed for their colleagues, for the boozing, blaspheming Welsh miners, for the sinful town of Lampeter. But above all, on every possible occasion, they prayed strenuously and publicly for the soul of the Vice-Principal. Ollivant found it irritating. He was not in need of such strenuous attentions. Already halfway to the gaiters, he felt no desire to be helped to grace by a wailing mob of students. 'There are those amongst us,' Prince had bellowed on one occasion, 'even in high places, who submit to the insinuations of carnal desire, and the solicitations of a self-indulgent and cross-defying flesh.' The Vice-Principal cursed inwardly. There was little else he could do. For Prince was in all other respects a model student. The wailing group of zealots came to be known as the Lampeter Brethren, and the Lampeter Brethren were the founder members of the Agapemone.

Of the six original brethren, we know that Lewis Price and George Robinson Thomas became disciples of the son of God, whereas Rees rejected him in 1843. The three others, John Lewis, Thomas Williams and Thomas Evans are lost in obscurity. They were an arrogant group, contemptuous of worldly authority, disdainful of their fellow students. Under Prince they became a positive menace to the establishment, for ever wailing and bellowing in outraged, prayerful discord at the sinful state of the college, remorselessly pursuing the Vice-Principal in a cacophony of prayer.

Prince ruled them with a rod of iron, dominating them so that their attitudes and behaviour reflected his personality. Confession was good for the soul, prayer a means of communicating with the Almighty, so he had them do both. He instructed them to meet daily in each other's rooms to lay bare their souls, to weep and pray for the perishing world and the Reverend Alfred Ollivant, who was never far from Prince's thoughts.

In spite of their behaviour, the Lampeter Brethren were not entirely rejected by authority. The college was a theological establishment. Many felt that prayer, providing it was liturgically correct, was the first duty and highest profit for those who seek after God. Gradually the Brethren increased in number. The postulants were not confined to undergraduates; Prince's emerging doctrine seduced a wide range of people, young and old, male and female.

Neither did the Lampeter Brethren confine themselves exclusively to prayer; Prince saw to that. On at least two occasions he managed to shatter the tranquil waters of the college in no uncertain manner.

The first instance was during a christening in the college chapel. The service had gone quietly without interruption, which is fairly remarkable, considering that Prince and the Brethren were present. But as the guests left the service, somebody, possibly Ollivant, unwisely suggested 'wetting the baby's head'. Prince rose up like the Angel of the Lord condemning the Israelites, ordering the guests to fall upon their knees instantly to pray for the soul of the child rather than drink its health. The Brethren, obedient as ever, flung themselves down in a gibbering group. The less zealous guests stood about uncertainly, in various degrees of embarrassment. The christening was not a success.

The second occasion was at another party, a little celebration thrown by the Vice-Principal to mark his advancement in the Church. For some reason, he was unwise enough to invite Prince and his associates to the gathering. Prince was passing through his 'Total Abstinence' period at the time, abhorring demon drink. Perhaps Ollivant was unaware of this, for he was certainly asking for trouble. At the height of the celebration, the son of God leapt at the Vice-Principal, dashed a glass of sherry clean out of his hand, admonished the astounded guests and departed to the hisses and boos of such of the sinners who were sufficiently sober to record their indignation.

And so it went on. The zealous Brethren of Lampeter, led by the son of God, charged about the college disturbing students and staff with abrasive fervour. Prince so thrived on conflict that nothing would pacify him. He saw himself as the Angel of the Lord, champion of the righteous, defender of the faith. Anybody bold enough to cross swords with him was immediately classified as a sinner. Those who persistently got in the way were referred to in his journal as, 'Poor O.', or 'poor Mr F.', or 'poor mother'. 'Poor O.', was a degenerate sinner, who submitted to the insinuations of carnal desire. 'Poor Mr F.' was very bitter to him personally: 'my God the mighty power of sin!' And 'poor mother' was sinfully incapable of understanding his purpose.

The Brethren increased and multiplied, entirely under the influence of their leader, whose will they obeyed without question. During the vacations he kept them in line, like St Paul with the Ephesians, writing long dogmatic epistles addressed to, 'My dearly beloved Brethren', exhorting them to pray continuously, instructing them to obey *His* will in every way. The will of God was beginning to get confused with the will of Prince; in time it would submerge completely.

The Reverend Alfred Ollivant, vice-principal of Lampeter. Resenting his easy superiority, wit and worldly manner, Prince set out to embarrass him in any way he could

Such frantic activity, in a lesser man, could have been academically disastrous. It was not so with H. J. Prince. He flourished at Lampeter, winning numerous scholarships and prizes, becoming fluent in Greek, expert in the scriptures. He was an undoubted scholar, with a ferocious energy. He divided his day into three parts. The morning was given to study, the afternoon to the Bible, the evening to prayer and contemplation. Rees in later years described Prince as having a heart that burned within him to be more and more devoted to God. According to him Prince could make 'mere mole-hills' from what would have been tremendous difficulties to others. Describing his personality, Rees continues—'I never knew one who was so independent of the censure and praise of his fellow-creatures; he walked straight on, without being either checked or impelled in his path by the good or bad opinions of those who knew him.' He would have made an admirable leader of men, a fine general perhaps, even a second Napoleon. It seems a pity that he chose to become God.

For that is exactly what he was to do at Lampeter. For him it was a time of trial, like Christ in the wilderness. At Lampeter the son of God finally rejected the temptations of the devil, renounced the flesh and secretly assumed the mantle of God. It was a slow, painful process, a subconscious transformation, like a moth emerging from a chrysalis. It was only years later that Prince discovered this astounding fact, long after he had become firmly established as the visible manifestation of God on earth.

Apart from the Brethren, who were for the most part willing to believe anything, few people at Lampeter had the insight to recognise the odour of sanctity surrounding the son of God. All they could see was a bigoted young firebrand. Fanatics such as the Lampeter Brethren tended to embarrass the established authority. They were in fact behaving dangerously like the dissenting enemy, against whom they were to be thrown. The Church was a respectable career, and parsons were not encouraged to rush about screaming Armageddon, and dashing glasses of sherry from the hands of their superiors. It simply was not done—not even in Wales.

Prince and his band of Brethren were becoming a menace. Ollivant could hardly cross the campus without being wailed at, and prayed for. He was barely safe in his own pulpit. The Brethren had, on more than one occasion, risen up during divine service to denounce the insinuations of carnal desire, disrupting the proceedings, and generating dissension amongst the congregation. Ollivant would have to dispose of the son of God before he lost his sanity, before they all lost their sanity. But how?

In all other respects Prince was a model student. Ollivant could hardly send him down for being pious or scholarly, neither could he justify expelling him for being zealous. It was a difficult situation. All the Vice-Principal could do was to wait patiently for the young man to graduate and then translate him, shovel him off to some remote unsuspecting parish, well out of range of Lampeter. Darkest Africa must have entered his thoughts; Prince with any luck might be cooked and eaten. But Prince showed no desire for missionary work in the sub-continent. There were sinners enough on his own doorstep; he need only step outside to be surrounded by perishing souls.

As the day of Prince's graduation drew nearer, Ollivant, now getting desperate, wrote off to his old friend Bishop Law of Bath and Wells. Ollivant wondered if his friend could find a suitably remote parish in Somerset, second only to darkest Africa. In this request he was fortunate. A curate was required in the village of Charlinch.

Charlinch was an excellent place in which Prince could fade into obscurity—or so it seemed. The village was remote, indifferent and tiny. It was situated in the Quantock foothills a few miles from Bridgwater. The parishioners consisted of indigenous farm labourers, ploughmen who preferred beer and skittles on a Sunday to church-going. It was a spiritual wilderness wherein a zealous young man such as Prince could preach himself to death and go unnoticed. The Rector spent most of his time in the Isle of Wight being ill, so that the parish was neglected, the church empty. It was an excellent proposition. Ollivant accepted with alacrity. The Bishop of Bath and Wells lived to regret it.

Prince, in the meantime, was assiduously cultivating Martha. It was a sensible thing to do, since she virtually kept him. During the term he bombarded her with long rambling letters about the state of her soul, issuing orders from above like Papal edicts. In the vacations he incarcerated the doting, enraptured victim in his bedroom and wooed her as ever with the Song of Solomon.

Mrs Prince looked on in dismay. She was getting old, worn out by constant friction and exhausted by the struggle to survive. His relationship with Martha was so unnatural that there were times when she doubted her son's sanity. She was alarmed by his extreme piety which was often morose, always fanatical. He seemed obsessed, remote, sometimes positively insane. When he was not incarcerated with Martha, he was stalking around Bath terrorising friends and relations, bellowing at them, painting lurid word pictures of hell and damnation, admonishing them furiously in the name of God.

Mrs Prince struggled on, and her efforts were not entirely in vain. Prince began to refer to her as 'Poor Mother' in his journal, a sure sign that she was not giving up easily.

At the beginning of 1838 the son of God turned his thoughts to the future. If he were to continue God's work on earth, he would need money, and nobody at Widcombe Crescent was getting any younger. Supposing 'poor mother' were to die? Supposing Martha were to die? What then? The Messiah would be virtually on the bread-line. A curate's stipend was not noticeably generous and he had a year or two more at Lampeter before he could take orders. Prince had no desire to be flung into penury, no desire to be forced back into the messy medical profession. The future must be secured. He consulted the Holy Ghost.

The Holy Ghost advised him to marry Martha. This was an astute move. Once Prince was legally joined to Martha her annuity would be his. As there was no Married Women's Property Act in those days, wives were the property of their husbands. With Martha's cash in his pocket, Prince could convert the faithless in comfort. He could, if he felt so inclined, follow the example of the other Messiah, cut himself off completely from his family and acknowledge only the family of God. That would be one in the eye for 'poor mother'. The Lord had spoken! The son of God hurried off to bestow his blessing upon *the fairest amongst women.*

Martha was overwhelmed. She had passed countless years of maidenhood waiting for Mr Right, and here was the son of God himself proposing holy wedlock. She remembered the Song of Solomon—*I rose up and opened to my Beloved; and my hands dripped with myrrh.* But the son of God had no intention of consummating the marriage; all he wanted was the cash. He was to find sexual fulfilment in other ways, with far more exciting partners. This was to be a spiritual marriage. Of course they would be legally joined as man and wife, that was essential. But there would be no 'hanky-panky', no sinful flesh-lusting intercourse. Prince was not interested in Martha's maidenhead, only her money. The unfortunate lady does not appear to have been ravished by the son of God, at least not physically.

They were married on the 10th of July 1838. Mrs Prince, a pale shadow of her former self, looked on bemused. The happy couple spent a brief honeymoon in Clifton, walking about the Downs. The rest of the time was spent in contemplation and religious discourse; a strange beginning to a strange marriage.

The honeymoon over, Prince returned to Lampeter, while Martha was left behind at Widcombe Crescent. Her presence at the college would only have distracted him from his studies. He did, however, invite her down for a weekend some time later to show her to the brethren. But she promptly fell ill and he was obliged to return her to Widcombe Crescent at considerable inconvenience. She never visited Lampeter again.

In the summer of 1840, to the evident relief of the Reverend Alfred Ollivant, the son of God passed his final examinations. Soon after, he was ordained, and accepted the curacy of Charlinch. The Vice-Principal relaxed with a glass of sherry.

Prince departed in triumph, the Holy Ghost strong within him. He had passed right through the middle of life and come out the other side of God. He was ready for the fray, ready to do battle with the sinners of Somerset. He summoned Martha from Widcombe Crescent and descended upon the little village of Charlinch.

It vexes my soul to see the thoughtless levity in those around me. One might think they were educating for the stage rather than the pulpit. My soul wearies of the filthiness of Horace.

H.J. Prince
Lampeter College, 14th March, 1836

A Very Odd Curate

It cannot be said that the two hundred or so inhabitants of Charlinch were noticeably moved by the arrival of the Messiah in their midst, nor did they flock in their multitudes to the little church on the hill. A few came to see the new curate at work, simply from curiosity. It was, on the whole, an unsatisfactory situation. Prince found himself casting pearls before swine. The word of God, frequently interrupted by gentle snores and the immoderate breaking of wind engendered by the excellent cider in the Lamb Inn, was simply not getting through.

The condition of the little church, God's house, was alarming. The roof threatened to fall in at a gust of wind, livestock had to be driven from the rickety, uncomfortable pews, and the graveyard was a veritable wilderness.

The Rector, the Reverend Samuel Starky, had neglected the parish for many years. Discouraged no doubt by lack of enthusiasm on the part of his flock, he had fled to the Isle of Wight, there to nourish one of the countless unnamed 'indispositions' that seemed to plague so many Victorians. He was not even aware that he had a curate. He would soon find out!

Prince, when it came to the point, did not lack energy. The recalcitrant sons of the soil would be brought to heel. The hand of God would seize them by the scruff of their necks, the wrath of God chastise their souls. By the time the Reverend H.J. Prince, with the assistance of the Holy Ghost, had set about this flock, they would indeed be sheep, baaing, bleating and begging for repentance.

He set to work with furious energy, throwing Martha into

the battle as well. They wrestled with the ploughmen, the ploughmen's wives, the ploughmen's children. They organised prayer groups, revivalist meetings, a Sunday school. They bellowed and roared, threatened and cajoled, with absolutely no effect. The rude labouring flock went on rudely labouring, the visitors from the pub continued to pass wind, and the Sunday school was a fiasco. The sinners of Charlinch were quite unmoved. Even the Holy Ghost became discouraged and Prince had to admit: 'There was not—with the exception of the Minister's own household—so much as one person either converted or awakened among all the people committed to his charge.'

Prince continued stubbornly; Martha, however, took to her bed. She was thoroughly worn out by evangelism coupled with housekeeping and the mounting impotent rage of her husband. It was too much for the frail old lady, and she began to fade.

For more than twelve months Prince fought on, pounding away at the sinful peasantry. The sum total of his efforts for that period amounted to tentative inquiries from three elderly ladies from another parish about the condition of their souls, and a very sick Martha. It was hardly a victory. Prince carried Martha back to Widcombe Crescent to keep his mother company, since she was ailing as well. It was a time of gloomy frustration; the tide was low, the spirit fading.

But help was at hand. The Holy Ghost, far from deserting his associate, sent him an angel from heaven in the person of the Reverend Samuel Starky, the absent rector of Charlinch.

To all intents and purposes irt was a miracle. The hand of God had reached out to Mr Starky in the Isle of Wight and drawn him miraculously to Charlinch.

The absent rector was expiring upon his death bed, nursed by his wife and sister, preparing to meet his maker, and abandoned by his doctors. He was fading fast, the end nigh. On the day of the miracle, the postman called to deliver a letter from a clerical friend in Bath. The letter contained a slip of paper, a printed copy of a sermon; the clerical friend had found it interesting.

Starky, committing himself to God, asked in a feeble voice if the sermon could be read to him before he slipped away and this was done. The result was miraculous. The words fell upon his soul like rain on parched ground, full of Grace, full of God. Before composing himself for the inevitable end, the dying man asked for the name of the preacher. It was the Reverend H.J. Prince, curate of Charlinch, his own parish. This was his own curate. Starky gave thanks to God for bringing such a wonderful pastor to his flock, then lay back to depart in peace. But he could not die. He just lay there thinking about the sermon, and the more he thought about the sermon, the less he wanted to die. His pulse beat quicker, his tongue was loosened. Strength returned to his limbs. He had been summoned, called as it were to God—to God on earth. The dying man leapt from his bed and rushed post-haste to Charlinch.

Starky was a weak, impressionable man, but he had virtues of birth, wealth and connexions in Somerset that were immensely useful to Prince. Through his grandmother, Lady Alicia Coventry, he was connected with half the peerage. His father, a renowned ecclesiastical scholar, had been rector of Charlinch before him and was well known in the county. He had all the privileges that wealth and breeding could supply, including th respect of the Established Church and the ear of the Bishop. He returned to Charlinch with his wife and sister Julia, to fall at once under the charismatic influence of his curate.

By now Prince firmly believed that he was the visible manifestation of God on earth. During his studies at Lampeter he had come upon the works of Gerhard Tersteegen, the German mystic and psalmist. Tersteegen believed that a longing for communion with God could be answered by totally absorbing the personality of the supplicant into the personality of God. For somebody like Prince it was meat and drink, supporting all his theories concerning his own total identification with the Holy Ghost. From consulting the deity on every occasion, it was only a short step to becoming the deity himself. Prince's body was weak, mere flesh, often racked with pain, tormented by ungodly thoughts and sinful desires. He would disown it, cast it off. It would remain, of course, for all to see. But it would not be *his* body; it would not be occupied by Henry James Prince—but by God. The process had been gradual, inevitable, evolving remorselessly from childhood until at Charlinch he was able to tell the gullible Starky, 'In me you see Christ in the flesh, Christ in my flesh.'

Starky believed him completely. From the first moment he stepped into his own rectory until the day of his death, he never doubted the divinity of his curate, such was Prince's influence over lesser men. Prince was helped along by Starky's miraculous recovery from impending death, although the story of this miracle comes from Starky himself and is open to conjecture. Everybody in those days appeared to be facing death, giving up the ghost one day, bouncing back the next. Prince did it habitually, so did Martha; it was obsessional.

With the return of its rector, the parish of Charlinch stirred reluctantly. A few more people began to trickle into church; a few more souls were claimed for the Holy Ghost. Starky never interfered with his curate's evangelical doings. He assumed a lesser place, befitting a lesser mortal, supporting the divine Prince by prayer and goodwill, but never presuming to meddle with his work. He joined the Lampeter

Brethren and lent them credence and authority. Prince still maintained his leadership over the group and dominated them. Starky had his sermons published and they were read widely in all the best places. The Lampeter Brethren became for a time respectable in the Church.

But Charlinch was slow, very slow. Five or six at the most were alarmed for their souls. Prince consulted the Holy Ghost once more.

It was a simple, highly effective ploy. It may have been quite unconsciously done on Prince's part, but the Holy Ghost was deeply involved. On one memorable Sunday, in October 1841, Prince mounted the pulpit to castigate the all too few assembled faithful and found himself 'quite shut up'. Now this was unusual. Prince as a rule found no trouble at all in thundering from the pulpit. When the wind was from the west he could be heard in the Lamb Inn on a Sunday morning. Prince 'shut up' was therefore curious. The congregation roused themselves from somnolence. The curate was gesticulating, waving his arms about and groaning dramatically. Some, thinking he was in the process of having a seizure, hurried to his assistance. But he waved them away and continued to claw the air, muttering and moaning. The faithful murmured anxiously. What on earth was going on? Should they summon a doctor? Was the curate going mad? The performance continued for some minutes, then stopped as suddenly as it started. The Holy Ghost, the curate announced, was not upon him; and he stalked out of the church. The congregation dispersed to their various abodes to mull over the proceedings.

The following Sunday they returned, bringing their friends and relatives, hoping for a repeat performance. They were not disappointed. Once more the curate mounted the pulpit, once more he suddenly became 'shut up', clawing the air, gasping, leaping about. It was fascinating. One or two enthusiastic worshippers even applauded. They had seldom enjoyed such entertainment at matins.

News of the mad curate of Charlinch swept across the county. People began to arrive in parties, drunks from Bridgwater, skittle teams on their way to Spaxton, house guests from country mansions, families in carts with picnics. The little church on the hill began to fill up rapidly. And it was not only the curate who supplied the increasing congregations with entertainment. The Rector could be seen leaping into the air; it was almost too good to be true. More and more people crammed into the church; advice and encouragement was offered from the pews. There were cheers and whistles, boos and catcalls. After the service they spilled out in brawling groups, charging down the hill to Spaxton to quench their thirst in the Lamb Inn. The regulars, resenting this intrusion, tried to repulse the advancing hordes by flinging empty flagons at them. Fighting broke out, windows were smashed and heads were cracked. It was good fun, better than skittles. And rugby had not yet arrived in the West Country.

Then, on one Sunday afternoon in November, during Evensong, the Holy Ghost returned to the Reverend H.J. Prince.

The church was unusually full. Prince mounted the pulpit to the expectant cheers of the congregation and to everyone's surprise began to preach. The sudden audacious transformation from one extreme to the other caught the congregation on the wrong foot. They fell silent, even the children in the gallery being shocked into stillness. It was a triumph; the Holy Ghost had chosen exactly the right occasion to return. Prince berated the gawping assembly forcefully, the spirit upon him, 'heavy as a hammer, sharper than a two-edged sword'.

A death-like stillness pervaded the church as the mad

curate spoke under the power of the Holy Ghost. Prince was a good preacher, at times brilliant. His powerful personality and sense of drama combined to hypnotise and drive his audience close to hysteria. That afternoon in Charlinch he surpassed himself. Such was the power of his intellect, the strength of his dominant character that men and women began to sob aloud. The Charlinch Revival had begun.

Prince was not slow to follow up his victory. For victory it had been. Not many that were present on that Sunday afternoon would forget. Some would fall away, preferring other entertainment; the majority of them would return to hear the new Prince. The people of Somerset have generally favoured the evangelical low Church as opposed to the high. They flocked to the colours of the dissenting Duke of Monmouth, to be cut down and mutilated by the Catholic King James. Memories are long; the people of Somerset who had come to laugh were happy to return to cry. Prince was never an inconsiderable man.

The work of grace continued, with the church full to overflowing. Prayer groups were formed, men on one night, women on another. The village of Charlinch became the centre of a quite furious and extremely noisy religious revival.

Having disposed of the adults, Prince turned his attention to the children. They were a turbulent set of little sinners, in much need of spiritual chastisement, corporal chastisement apparently having little effect. Prince, so exasperated by his lack of success in the Sunday school, had virtually abandoned them to the devil. They were such hardened sinners, he had determined to 'speak to them no more of Jesus'.

Now that the Holy Ghost had returned, he decided to try again. He recalled the Sunday school, convinced that it would surrender to the spirit, as had the adults in the church.

In the event it did, with devastating effect.

The tiny parish church at Charlinch where Prince was seized by the Holy Ghost. His curacy was terminated when revivalist fervour led to riots in the parish

About fifty boys and girls of assorted ages were herded into the single room of the little school next to the church. The event is recorded in some detail in Prince's pamphlet, *The Charlinch Revival*. It is worth repeating, if only to give the reader some idea of the self-satisfaction and terrifying ferocity of Victorian Evangelism.

Dec 19.—On this day the 'revival' in the school commenced. The Lord directed the minister to announce from the pulpit that, if any persons would send their children to the school-room that evening, he would lecture them: accordingly about fifty were assembled. The word spoken was at first very solemn, but in a few minutes the Holy Ghost came on the minister with the most tremendous power, so that the word of the Lord was really like fire. About twenty of the children were pierced to the heart by it, and appeared to be in great distress; but the bigger boys still continued unmoved, and some of them even disposed to laugh. In a short time, however, the word reached them too, and they were smitten to the heart with the most dreadful conviction of their sins and danger; it appeared as if the arrows of the Almighty had pierced their very veins; indeed, the Lord really seemed to have made the mouth of the minister like a sharp sword; so tremendous was the power of the word spoken. In about ten minutes the spectacle presented by the school-room was truly awful: out of fifty children present there were not so many as ten that could stand upright: boys and girls, great and small together, were either leaning against the wall quite overcome by their feelings of distress, or else bowed down with their faces hidden in their hands, and sobbing in the severest agony: it appeared positively as if the Spirit of God was breaking their hearts into pieces like a potter's vessel. The most heart-felt anguish was written on almost every countenance that could be seen; whilst some of them looked as though they were inwardly wrung by the extent of the agony they endured. During the prayer that followed, the impression made by the Spirit became still deeper, till the walls of the school-room quite resounded with the sobs and cries of the children kneeling on the floor; and for some time after the minister had ceased to pray, they continued where they were, not weeping, but literally deeply wailing.

It would be impossible to express in words the awful sense of God's presence and power which was felt by those that were in the school-room on this occasion; it made the hearts of even the converted quail and compelled them to shrink into Christ for refuge; even they 'did exceedingly fear and quake.'

Who can possibly resist the conviction that the hand of the Lord had done this. What power less than that of the Holy Ghost could have wrought conviction, and produced humiliation such as this?

There is probably some convincing modern psychological explanation for the revival in the school. Mass-hysteria perhaps, similar to that affecting 'teeny-boppers' at pop concerts. But there is no doubt that Prince and the converted considered it to be the work of God. It is interesting to read, farther on in Prince's account, that not all the children were struck down. Indeed one child, a boy, was totally unaffected by the power of the spirit and stood upright amongst his howling playmates, 'with a vacant stare of stupid astonishment upon his face'.

The revival continued unabated, and people flocked to Charlinch to hear the word of God from the mad curate. The Lampeter Brethren, summoned to assist in the conversion of souls, turned up in force. News of the revival spread far and wide, fluttering the frocks and gaiters of the established Church, ruffling an occasional cassock. But Samuel Starky had the ear of the Bishop; the Rector of Charlinch was well connected and a gentleman—there was no need for alarm.

But Samuel Starky was converted and, in any case, had no more influence over Prince than he would have over the Almighty. The establishment had every cause for alarm. The curate had got the bit between his teeth, the Holy Ghost advising him to do all sorts of strange things. The evening meetings, for instance, were becoming scandalous, especially the women's evening. Attendance had increased immensely and the sound of shrill voices raised in revivalist passion was beginning to be misconstrued. One passion was very like another, and the Reverend H.J. Prince was undoubtedly attractive to women.

The greatest and by far the most rash of all Prince's impulsive actions arrived when the Holy Ghost advised him to separate the wheat from the chaff.

This winnowing of the harvest had immediate and disastrous consequences. Prince in his wisdom, like the pig in *Animal Farm*, decided that from the converted there were some more converted than others. This was undoubtedly true, many of the faithful packing the church being by no means 'hot for Christ'. They had come for the entertainment, and they were at best lukewarm. However that had not stopped them from turning up, or dropping their pennies into the plate. So when Prince announced that only the righteous would be admitted to the services, they naturally assumed he was referring to them. He was not, and they were livid.

Prince selected the faithful personally, which was a dangerous thing to do. It was even more dangerous when he sternly sent the lukewarm about their business, forbidding them to enter the church or attend the prayer meetings. He was extremely fastidious in his choice, dividing up families into saints and sinners and even more dangerously classifying most of the influential local gentry as sinners. Fury raged in Somerset, the wheat becoming sanctimonious and superior, the chaff black with rage and charged with aggression. As factions warred against each other, wheat and chaff clashed in the streets of Bridgwater. Husbands beat their wives for being faithful—at least that was original. Boys and girls quarrelled with their parents, servants with their masters. The local drunks and bully-boys joined in and fought everybody impartially. The country for miles around Charlinch was in turmoil. The Bishop stirred in his palace; all was not well.

George Henry Law, Bishop of Bath and Wells, was elderly. His greatest desire was to be left in peace to enjoy the tranquil comfort of his beautiful moated palace at Wells. Sounds of fury, the clamour of embattled Christians, the outraged shrieks of rejected gentry, penetrated the sacred haven, disturbing the old man's drowsy contemplation. Agitated clerics scuttled in and out of the palace bearing tidings of religious frenzy in Charlinch; purple-faced landowners on the verge of epilepsy hammered on his doors. It appeared that the diocese was embroiled in a kind of Holy War fomented by a lunatic curate from Lampeter.

Bishop Law, disturbed into unaccustomed action, summoned the Reverend Samuel Starky to Wells. Starky, completely besotted by Prince, firmly believing him to be the Almighty, must have convinced the Bishop that he was very nearly as demented as his curate. Nevertheless, the aged prelate, perhaps because of the Rector's connexions, contented himself with a few words of fatherly advice. Possibly the Almighty in the person of Mr Prince would be more useful in some other diocese. The Church in Somerset did not really want a second Messiah; one was quite sufficient. He advised Starky to remove his abrasive curate to fresh fields and pastures new.

Starky conveyed the suggestion to Prince, who ignored it. No Bishop was going to give orders to the Holy Ghost. Prince had arrived in Charlinch on intimation from above. He would leave when the Spirit moved him to leave, and not before. He continued winnowing the wheat from the chaff.

In the midst of the turmoil, Martha gave up the ghost and died. She had served her master as best she could, tending his needs, supplying him with cash, and nursing him through numerous indispositions. But she had not been equal to the pressures of revivalist warfare, and never thrived outside the confines of No. 5 Widcombe Crescent.

Prince buried her without ceremony and almost immediately married Starky's sister, Julia. The speed of the exercise surprised even the Rector. Martha had been the Beloved one, the fairest amongst women. How could the Almighty cast her memory aside with such alacrity? He was barely on nodding terms with Julia, hardly aware of her presence in the Rectory, and now he was taking her in marriage; strange indeed.

The chaff had a field day—it was indecent. The funeral baked meats were indecently furnishing the marriage table. Besides, the second Mrs Prince was hardly more desirable than the first. She was no beauty, would not see fifty again and had little to offer, apart from an annuity. Ah! the annuity. They drew their own conclusions.

Prince ignored everything and everybody, except Julia. Not that he paid her much attention either. It was the will of God; they were married by order from above and that was that. The annuity had nothing to do with it. God's work on earth continued in Charlinch. Julia, rather more vigorous and every bit as doting as Martha, took her place as the fairest among women. It seems unlikely that they had sexual relations. Prince was no more attracted by her than he had been by Martha. There is no doubt he would have 'entered her door' had the Spirit moved him, but he seemed to prefer the young girls of the Sunday school, and the converted ladies of Charlinch.

The ladies' meetings and the Sunday school had been a huge success. The Holy Ghost, knee-deep in repentant wailing women and children, reigned supreme. The converts were fashioned into vessels for the Almighty, offering their bodies and souls for his exclusive use. Whilst this satisfied Prince it did nothing to placate the wrath of the chaff who were, in many cases, the husbands and lovers of the converted.

On the 4th of May 1842 Bishop Law, driven to distraction, revoked Prince's licence to preach within the diocese of Bath and Wells. Once again he was 'shut up', this time by a mere mortal. Prince was outraged. If the Church of England and its pettifogging prelates failed to recognise the hand of God in its midst, then the hand of God would be withdrawn. Without it the church would surely flounder and sink in a morass of perishing sinners.

Prince consulted the Holy Ghost and for the first time in his life sought the advice of lesser mortals in the guise of the Lampeter Brethren who strongly advised their leader to remain within the Church. His position was strong because many of his sermons had been published, thanks to Starky. He was not without admirers within the establishment. Moreover most of the brethren had, by now, been ordained and had obtained livings. If he left at this point, they would be faced with an agonising decision.

Prince and the Holy Ghost pondered long and earnestly. They were well aware of the weakness of the brethren, not deluding themselves that, if given the final choice, the brethren would stick with the bread and butter. They were also aware that, whilst Starky remained Rector of Charlinch, Prince could put one of his creatures into the curacy without the slightest difficulty. Prince was directed to remain within the Church for the time being.

The question now arose as to what the divine pair should do. The parish church was closed, at least to Prince. Presumably the Holy Ghost could enter from time to time, and even-

George Henry Law who, as Bishop of Bath and Wells, was driven to revoke Prince's licence to preach in the diocese

tually they would have to find a living in another diocese. But Julia had an annuity, enough to keep her husband comfortably solvent and more. Bishop Law might be able to prevent the word of God from being heard on church property, but he could not stop it being heard altogether. There were other places within the village.

One of the converted was a civil engineer, employed on the Bristol and Exeter railway line, whose name was William Cobbe. Cobbe, apart from Starky, was one of Prince's wealthiest triumphs. He was the designer and builder of the Agapemone in later years, and a very useful man indeed. He promptly set to work building a small meeting place for the converted in the valley, about a mile and a half from Charlinch Hill. Where the money came from is not known; probably from Starky and Cobbe himself. Certainly Prince contributed nothing—he never did. His approbation was sufficient payment for the converted.

One of the original Lampeter Brethren, the Reverend George Robinson Thomas was appointed to the curacy in Prince's place, and the revival continued very much as before.

But in spite of having his own church Prince felt restless. The wheat had been winnowed from the chaff, the district gleaned dry. There was a trickle of repentant sinners coming in, but it was not exactly a deluge. The first fine careless rapture of revivalist fervour was fading. The village was beginning to settle down. It was time to move on.

The Spirit came on him with power. He did not preach; but the Holy Ghost preached by him. The word was not vehement, and far too solemn to be violent; but it was searching as fire, heavy as a hammer, and sharper than a two-edged sword. A death-like stillness pervaded the whole church, so very solemn that one almost seemed afraid to breathe lest something should be disturbed by it. Several men and women sobbed aloud; the heads of most dropped on their breast; the hearts of all were awe-struck.

Reverend H.J. Prince, 'The Charlinch Revival'
December 1840

Charisma in Brighton

By the summer of 1842, Prince claimed one hundred and two perishing sinners brought to God. Considering the size of the parish, this was a remarkable achievement. Prince also claimed that his flock of converts remained faithful in the face of the most 'awful persecution'. The women and children suffered extreme harassment. Frequently abused, often physically beaten by the ungodly, they clung heroically to their new-found faith. They would trudge miles through the lanes in the most inclement weather to attend Prince's prayer meetings. The converts came from all over Somerset, converging three times a week on the little chapel in the valley below Charlinch Hill.

But Prince was restless; a mere one hundred and two souls was a drop in the ocean. St Peter, speaking under the Spirit, had collected three thousand converts in one single day. If *he* could do it, so could Prince and better. But he would have to move on.

Starky provided the opportunity and Prince seized it. The rector had a clerical friend at Clare, in Suffolk, who had informed him that a young man was required for ministerial duties in the parish of Stoke, a village not far from Halstead. It was larger than Charlinch, and contained one of the finest churches in East Anglia. It seemed ideal. The Holy Ghost thought so too. Prince accepted the appointment and moved across to Suffolk, taking Julia with him. He was once more established in the Church of England. It would not last for long.

The people of Suffolk, apart from their dialect, are not very different from the people of Somerset. Stoke was a country parish like Charlinch, but with a rather larger population of farmers and labourers.

Within a year Prince succeeded in setting the village and surrounding district into a blaze of revivalist frenzy. The usual battles raged between the 'wheat and the chaff'. The streets of Stoke and Halstead rang to the battle cries of saints and sinners. Large parties and conducted tours of the battlegrounds were organised. Package deals were set up which included a free visit to the parish church to witness the bellowings of the mad curate. The locals thoroughly enjoyed themselves; it was enormous fun. The pubs emptied during Matins and Evensong, and a good time was had by all—except by the establishment in general, and his Grace the Bishop of Ely in particular.

Dr Allen, Bishop of Ely, was a tolerant man, even liberal in terms of the period. He had treated the ferocious young zealot with tact, patiently oiling troubled waters, placating his gibbering colleagues, pacifying the ungodly. But there were limits even to his patience, and having refereed the bloody contest for nearly two years, he was finally obliged to send off the principal offender. Prince was summoned to the palace at Ely, and requested to take his services elsewhere.

This was the last straw. The establishment of the Church of England was a bunch of blind, ignorant bigots. First Ollivant, then Law and now Allen. Prince rose up and denounced the lot of them as men of straw, images of clay, drinkers of port wine and claret. The Church and all its pompous prelates could go to the devil—they were, he considered, halfway there already. Prince was the visible manifestation of God on earth, the Holy Ghost, how could *he* toil in the same vineyard as these sinful mortals? He summoned the faithful to Stoke to announce the parting of the ways.

The faithful arrived with tidings of no great joy. Things

Dr Allen, Bishop of Ely. Like Bishop Law, Dr Allen was driven to banishing Prince from his diocese. Prince considered both of them to be men of straw, images of clay and drinkers of port wine and claret

had not gone well for the Lampeter Brethren during the past year. Charlinch had fallen, Starky had been suspended from all clerical duties and Thomas was on the verge of following suit. Rees, the seafaring man, the first of the faithful, had turned against them. This was the unkindest cut of all.

The moment of Rees's disillusion had come during and after a meeting of the brethren that Prince had called in Swansea. Rees had suspected for some time that their leader had been gradually assuming the mantle of God. But he admired him greatly, read his sermons and pamphlets, was impressed by his undoubted scholarship and, to some extent, his philosophy. He had given his friend the benefit of the doubt. The meeting at Swansea had been held to consider how the brethren could increase their usefulness in the ministry. Minutes had been taken, and it was all very democratic. But afterwards Prince had walked off with the minutes in his pocket. A week or two later the same minutes were published and distributed to the faithful. They bore no relationship to the original, being in fact a series of decrees, orders from above, and not at all democratic. Moreover Prince ordered the brethren to fast at least once a week. According to Rees this was an unreasonable suggestion because some of the brethren were not in the best of health. The matter had been discussed and recorded at the meeting. Prince's version of the minutes omitted to mention this. Fasting, according to him, was mandatory, and to disobey was contrary to the will of God; the culprit would be excommunicated.

It was enough for Rees. He greatly admired his friend, appreciating his spiritual nobility; but nothing would persuade him that he was God. Prince had gone too far. Consequently Rees left the brethren. Prince condemned him to everlasting perdition and they started a bitter war of words that was to last for the rest of their lives.

Although the fortunes of the Lampeter Brethren were beginning to waver, Prince was not discouraged. His ministry at Stoke had not been wasted. Sinners had come to God in useful numbers, some of them wealthy. Moreover he had made a notable conquest, probably the most important conquest of his career.

Josias Nottidge was a retired London merchant, living at Rosehill, near Clare. He was extremely wealthy, bucolic and very old. He was also burdened with a wife and five unmarried daughters. The daughters—Harriet, Agnes, Clara, Cornelia and Louisa—were middle-aged spinsters, the youngest being forty. They were God-given material for Prince's apostolic prowess. Since he 'specialised' in this type of frustrated woman, he found no difficulty whatsoever in bringing all five of them to God; had he so inclined he could just as easily have brought them to bed! They adored him, worshipped him, wilted for him.

The same cannot be said for the parents of the five ageing maidens. Mrs Nottidge refused to have anything to do with the Saviour, and old Nottidge blasphemed vigorously at the mention of his name. This did Prince's cause no end of good. The more old Nottidge cursed and swore, the more the maidens worshipped and wilted. The more vigorously he blasphemed, the worse for his health. Sooner or later he would collapse and die—and that was very much what Prince desired. The spinsters stood to inherit the sum of six thousand pounds apiece from their father's estate, a small fortune in total. Prince sensed the possibilities and cultivated the ladies with all the charm at his disposal.

The immediate problem, however, was what to do next. Prince, in his usual manner, had managed to replace himself at Stoke with one of his disciples, the Reverend Lewis Price. Price, though, would not last long. He was already in conflict with the establishment and likely to go the same way as

Starky, Thomas and Prince himself. But all was not lost. God Almighty had not moved his son to marry Julia Starky for nothing. She had enough cash to see them through, as did her brother. Between them they could supply enough working capital to keep the Holy Ghost in business without the help of the Church of England. Prince consulted the deity—divine guidance was generally sound.

Divine guidance decreed that both Prince and Starky should set up on their own. Starky would spread the word in Weymouth and Prince would convert fashionable Brighton.

The milieus were not chosen at random. Weymouth and Brighton were both renowned watering places, well stocked with wealthy old ladies; each town offered fertile ground for Prince and his disciple. Starky had relations at Weymouth, and certainly connexions in Dorset. He hired a house in Belfield Terrace and set to work.

Prince rode down to Brighton. He rented a hall in Windsor Street, named it the Adullam Chapel and quickly filled it with the usual crowd of converts, scoffers and the curious. Now that he was free from the established Church he felt able to justify himself as the visible manifestation of God. He did not, as yet, feel confident enough to announce it from the roof tops, but implied in no uncertain terms that the Saviour of the world was about to make his appearance. This intrigued the dowagers and idle rich of Brighton, who found the Adullam Chapel a change from the tea rooms and gossip on the Grand Parade.

A riveting preacher, Prince became fashionable. His message was direct and deliciously hair-raising. The Holy Ghost was coming in earthly form; the world was in its last dying days; sinners would roast in hell; only the righteous would survive. Most of the congregation had heard it all before. Armageddon has always been popular amongst revivalists among whom the world is always coming to an end.

But Prince was different; he had style, charisma, personality. The rich old ladies shuddered deliciously and wondered if they were right in thinking that their divine preacher *was* the Holy Ghost, as he seemed to imply.

There was no shortage of converts in Brighton; on the contrary there were almost too many. Prince was faced with a dilemma. He saw no reason why he should go to the trouble of converting the ungodly, only to see them escape the moment his back was turned. He needed somewhere to put them, somewhere secure. The Adullam Chapel was all right in its way but it was not large and it was not secluded. He could see the possibilities of a safe, private, enclosed establishment—a sort of monastery and convent combined. He saw no advantage in segregating the sexes, which would defeat his purpose. He wanted to put the faithful to work, the men to toil and the women... ? He consulted the Holy Ghost.

It was at this point that the 'awful heresy' Rees foresaw took hold of the Reverent H.J. Prince. For he abandoned Brighton to the devil and went across to join Starky in Weymouth. Had the Almighty advised him to stay in Sussex as a preacher, a pastor, a minister of the word, he might well have established a large and powerful following, even a new denomination. But he did not. Some people would say that Prince was not entirely interested in being a mere pastor, that his real desires were carnal, that he wished to get amongst the faithful women, to indulge in sinister sexual excesses. Prince ignored such critics and went off to Weymouth.

The reason for his going appears to be the large rented house in Belfield Terrace. Starky had collected some of the faithful together, and Belfield Terrace was large enough to accommodate them and would serve as an interesting experiment in the type of monastic living that Prince envisaged.

Belfield Terrace was an experimental Agapemone, a mini Abode of Love.

The concept of the Abode of Love was not original. Similar experiments had been condemned by the early Christian Church as sinful, pagan and dangerous. They had started as love feasts and quickly degenerated into orgies. Religion and sex can be closely related, as Prince well knew.

In the first half of the nineteenth century, whilst Prince was languishing at Guy's Hospital, a Frenchman, Prosper Enfantin, had experimented with a similar set up at Menilmonyant. But this was French, frivolous and dedicated to Venus. Enfantin was arrested in 1832 for outraging public morals, but nobody took him seriously and he was released. The Americans, of course, had bigger and better Abodes. The Mormons, the Shakers and numerous other sects were indulging in all sorts of spiritual extravaganza.

Prince had his own ideas; inevitably stemming from the Song of Solomon, and just as inevitably entirely for the benefit of Prince. Since this was a Victorian establishment, sex would be prohibited, at least amongst lesser mortals. The married faithful would live apart, men and women strictly segregated. The Abode of Love did not mean, as it seemed to imply, unlimited sexual freedom. Love at Belfield Terrace, and later at Spaxton, was to be spiritual. In the course of time Prince constructed an elaborate system of Angels and Archangels, a celestial hierarchy promoting and demoting the faithful at will, according to their favour in his eyes and the cash at their disposal. For this was to be a commercial as well as a spiritual venture. Not even the Holy Ghost could build an earthly paradise on faith alone.

The house at Belfield Terrace was the beginning of bliss for H.J. Prince. The faithful meekly accepted his dogma and submitted joyfully to his will. Whether he started to indulge his sexual excesses at this point is not known. He had not, as yet, publicly announced his transformation into the son of God and he was actively concerned with financing his future grandiose intentions. On the other hand material for sexual indulgence was available. He was surrounded by obedient and submissive women, many of them physically attractive. He may have exercised *Droit de Seigneur* over those early converts as he certainly did in later years.

Belfield Terrace was a reward for labouring in the vineyard. But it was far too small and not nearly secluded enough for Prince's purposes. He needed to expand. The son of God could hardly reign over a rented house. He must have a place in the country, away from prying eyes: a great house surrounded by walls, to keep the ungodly out and the faithful in. He thought of Charlinch and Spaxton nestling in the valley below. *A fountain of gardens, a well of living waters, and streams from Lebanon*, it was ideal. He would build his paradise in Spaxton, in the lovely valley running to the Quantock Hills, *let my Beloved come into his garden, and eat his pleasant fruits.*— There was only one problem: money. The Holy Ghost rolled up his sleeves.

The Blessed Spirit was personally united to him; he was THE HOLY GHOST PERSONIFIED.

Thus, the false principle of 1837 gradually conducted him to the awful heresy of 1843.

'The Rise and Progress of the Heresy of the Reverend H.J. Prince'
Pamphlet published by Arthur Augustus Rees, 1846

The Spiritual Marriages

The word went forth. The highways and byways of Dorset rang to the cries of Prince and his disciples as did village halls, back rooms in public houses, barns and backyards. Wherever two or three could be gathered together, the revivalists preached.

'The world is in its latter day,' they roared; 'the Day of Judgement is at hand.' It was the old story of Armageddon, the destruction of mankind—'A great and strong wind will rend the mountains and break in pieces the rocks before the Lord. But the Lord will not be in the wind. After the wind there will be an earthquake, but the Lord will not be in the earthquake. And the souls of the sinners will tremble at the discovery of their dreadful danger, and the certainty of their everlasting destruction.' It was uncompromising, stark and extraordinarily effective.

This sort of preaching had great appeal in the midst of the nineteenth century. There was little other entertainment to be had. Prince could whip up hysteria in much the same ways pop groups do today. He had done it in Somerset and Suffolk, and now he was doing it in Dorset. But this time he had a second message. 'Behold he cometh!' he announced again and again. Whenever their master paused for breath, one or other of his disciples would leap to his feet to announce the imminent arrival of the Lamb of God. Yes, the world was in its latter day, they seemed to say; the sinners will be destroyed in the burning fiery furnace. But for those who believed there was hope, the Lamb of God was about to descend from heaven, to appear in earthly form.

And then came the crunch! The very essence, the whole carefully generated purpose of the exercise—money.

'In the day of wrath all property would be dirt,' they told their congregations. 'When the world should be burning to ashes and the skies melting, where would be the use of their flocks and herds, their corn and fruit, their rank and state? Could they ride on horses to the throne of Grace? Could they drive in chariots to the judgement-seat?' No, of course not. There was only one answer, 'Sell everything for the Lord. He is coming, he is even now descending from heaven; he will provide.'

The Lord, when he did arrive, provided nothing in terms of hard cash; it was the converted who produced that. Farmers sold their land, craftsmen their tools, grocers their stock. Rich and poor alike realised their assets and threw their money into a common pool to await the coming of the Lamb of God. And the Lamb of God was about to reveal himself in the earthly form of the Reverend H.J. Prince.

The revelation of the son of Man took place in the Assembly Rooms of the Royal Hotel at Weymouth. The rooms were crammed with supplicants, driven into a state of near-hysteria by the constant attentions of Prince and his disciples, waiting nervously for the miraculous transformation. They were not disappointed. Prince, with his usual fine sense of drama, entered to a flourish of trumpets. He was surrounded by his disciples and a retinue from Belfield Terrace. Hymns of praise lifted the roof of the Assembly Rooms: 'Behold he Cometh', 'Behold he is amongst us!' The Lamb of God blessed the congregation and announced that the day of grace was past, that the lost were lost—the saved were saved. Only those who received the Reverend H.J. Prince as the son of God would be snatched from the holocaust. Once more the wheat would be winnowed from the chaff. Those prepared to sacrifice their all would be wheat, the

Royal Hotel, Weymouth, scene of the Revelation of the Son of Man

rest chaff; and the chaff was doomed to the burning fiery furnace.

Prince claimed over five hundred souls brought to God on that occasion. Dixon puts it at about a hundred aged spinsters, a few children and perhaps as many men. In any case, it was a goodly number, and the son of God was able to open an account to accommodate the price of salvation. The account was in the name of H.J. Prince. One of the converts brought to God that day was a widow and her daughter from Weymouth. The widow's name was Paterson. Her daughter, a child of five, was to grow into a delectable, nubile adolescent.

In his essay 'Justification', Aldous Huxley writes, 'There is no dogma so queer, no behaviour so eccentric or even outrageous, but a group of people can be found to think it divinely inspired.' This was very much the case with Prince, and Huxley is referring to him specifically. But he also implies that it is universal, timeless and this is borne out by the numerous way-out sects that have existed recently, Charles Manson being a particularly horrific example. It was no different in the nineteenth century, and may even have been easier for revivalists like Prince. Victorian Christian dogma was extremely ferocious, especially towards children, who were threatened with hell upon almost every occasion as punishment for their sins. One only has to read *Jane Eyre* to discover that.

So it is not all that surprising to find quite a substantial number of frightened, gullible people accepting Prince's dogma of hell and damnation. It is also not surprising, considering the healthy fear of God engendered by Victorian teaching, that people could be persuaded to buy their way out.

When it comes to parting the faithful from their worldly goods, Prince had no equal. He stood head and shoulders above Starky, Price, Thomas and the other disciples. He preached his own gospel, based on his own logic. His knowledge of the scriptures was formidable, and backed up by evident scholarship. Coupled with fiery rhetoric, it amounted to near genius.

Many who heard him preach were seduced in spite of themselves; they were not all gullible. Prince had the ability to win over sceptics by sheer rhetorical skill and personality. Those who came to jeer often left converted. Those who came for comfort were seldom disappointed, and almost all of them were relieved of their money.

The gospel according to Brother Prince was briefly this—

God created the earth, he also created man. But man is weak, sinful, and flesh-loving. So God is obliged to punish him from time to time, to bring him to judgement. Thus we have the fall of man, the flood, the plagues of Egypt and the destruction of Jerusalem. However, God is merciful. Before each particular day of judgement he sends a messenger to warn mankind of its folly and to save the righteous from impending doom. This messenger comes in human form and is perfect in his generation. Adam was the first, Noah the second, Abraham the third, Christ the fourth, H.J. Prince the fifth.

The doctrine, such as it is, flows from an omniscent pattern of judgement followed by a period of dispensation, followed by judgement. The spirit in human form, perfect in his generation, acts as a kind of link-man, joining one period of dispensation to another. He winnows the wheat from the chaff and the righteous from the unrighteous, discarding the one and saving the other to start a new covenant with God. It was a useful doctrine for Prince, neatly justifying the construction of the Agapemone as a sort of Noah's Ark, as well as his own pretensions to divinity.

How much of this he believed himself is not known. He

certainly took it very seriously, writing long, waffling, incomprehensible tomes which endlessly justified his own deceit and described his slow crucifixion and resurrection in terms of his stomach ailments and operation. But always behind the fervour there lies a hard, practical, commercial sense. The rambling books are directed more at the faithful, who might be wavering, than at the sceptical faithless, whom he despised. The transformation had been a gradual process following a pattern of prayer, self-denial, and obedience to the will of God. Most commendable; what it led to was not quite so commendable, as Rees had realised. He could see the advancing heresy, see that the will of God would inevitably submit to the will of Prince to become a useful justification of his friend's outrageous desires. Rees left, while he still had his sanity, and though most of the others stayed on, many of them regretted it later. But not all. This must be said. The Agapemone functioned for over a hundred years, and people lived and died behind its walls, firmly believing in the divinity of its founder and his successors.

If the transformation had been gradual, haphazard and at times tentative, the revelation was certainly none of these things. On the contrary, it was a well planned, nicely timed publicity stunt. Prince was quite unscrupulous when it came to money, although he was always careful to work within the law. Cobbe, the engineer, had already been sent down to Spaxton and negotiations were under way. The Agapemone was not just a presumptious dream. The faithful would see to that.

Cash poured in to the common fund. Prince had declared himself the saviour of the faithful, the select few. He would lead them to salvation, to grace and safety in the Agapemone; but they must pay a price. In the day of wrath all property would be dirt, when the Almighty would scarcely be impressed by frightened sinners brandishing consols and debentures before the judgement seat. You could not take it with you and you could not leave it behind to be consumed by the burning fiery furnace. Better to sell everything, pay the cash into the fund and buy salvation in the Agapemone.

In order to encourage philanthropy, Prince rewarded the principal donors with various titles and positions in his celestial entourage. For example, when a certain Hotham Maber with his four sisters contributed no less than ten thousand pounds, the lucky man was created Angel of the Seventh Seal. He appeared to be most honoured by this favour. His sisters do not merit a mention, perhaps being favoured in other ways. If Prince could be generous to the opulent, he could be very different to the less well-heeled amongst the faithful. Recalcitrant or penniless faithful were castigated unmercifully, reduced to the status of unpaid servants, and put to work in the stables and pigsties. There was no room for paupers in the Agapemone, except perhaps amongst some of the younger women with other things to offer.

Prince had other ways of raising money which were less subtle, more direct, but equally effective. He would simply send for it. 'The Lord had need of fifty pounds. Amen.'—Who could refuse such a demand, or who would dare? The demand usually arrived in the form of a note tucked under the victim's plate at meal times. The terrified convert would invariably pay up, rather than face the wrath of God and a period in the pigsties.

The money poured in. Cobbe set to work designing and building the new Agapemone. Two hundred acres of land had been secured in the Spaxton valley below the parish church of Charlinch. But yet more money was needed. The immediate faithful had been bled white; Starky had contributed every penny he possessed, Julia also. Price and Thomas were penniless, and Prince and the Holy Ghost had no intention of squandering their own capital for their greater glory.

But divine providence was at hand. The aged blaspheming sinner, Josias Nottidge, had recently died. As expected, the old man had left his daughters the sum of six thousand pounds each. Prince consulted the Holy Ghost.

What emerged amounted to genius. Three of the five sisters, Harriet, Angus and Clara, had followed Prince to Brighton and from thence to Weymouth. Dominated, they were submissive, compliant and adoring. They would do exactly as they were told.

In the ordinary way the three sisters would simply have been commanded to place their windfalls into the common fund. They would have complied, except perhaps Agnes who was a little less pliant than her sisters. But this was not ordinary. In the first place it was a large sum, in the second place the maidens were unmarried and, last but not least, the surviving members of the family were keeping a jealous eye on Harriet, Agnes and Clara. Any sudden movement of capital to Prince's favour would have been contested. The Nottidge family were suspicious of the Heavenly Host and quite prepared to do battle, if given the opportunity.

But there was another way of securing the spinsters' capital for the glory of God. Simple, legal and utterly irrevocable—marriage.

In the summer of 1846 Prince led a party of the faithful over the hills from Weymouth to Spaxton. The house in Belfield Terrace was getting uncomfortably crowded, the Agapemone was nearing completion and could provide accommodation for the overflow. The party in transit included the three Nottidge sisters.

They broke the journey at Taunton, spending the night in two hotels. Prince accommodated himself in style at Gyle's, while the women, including the three Nottidge sisters, put up in rather less style at the Castle Inn. The following morning, at an early hour, probably before breakfast when she would not have been at her best, Agnes received a summons to the presence. Obediently she put on her bonnet and hurried over.

The Lamb of God, flanked on one side by his wife Julia and on the other by Samuel and Mrs Starky confronted the lady in one of the more expensive private rooms of the hotel. There was an air of imperious solemnity that must have struck awe into the empty stomach of Agnes Nottidge as she entered the apartments of the Holy Ghost.

'Agnes,' Prince announced in a grave voice, 'God is about to confer on you a special blessing.' Agnes fluttered. Prince continued, 'A great blessing is to be bestowed on you Agnes, but before I tell you what it is, you must give me your word to obey the Lord and accept his gift.' Agnes duly complied; there was little else she could do. One simply did not refuse gifts from God in the presence of Beloved.

'Then,' Prince continued firmly, 'in a few days time you will be united in marriage to brother Thomas.' There followed what could only be described as a 'pregnant pause'. Agnes was not sure if she wanted brother Thomas, even as a gift from God. She hardly knew him, was barely on nodding terms with him, and yet here was Beloved calmly announcing almost instant matrimony. What on earth was the Holy Ghost up to? Had he gone mad?

'Amen,' Prince concluded. The audience was over. Agnes, however, was the more spirited of the three sisters. 'This is so sudden, so unexpected,' she managed to stutter as she was swept towards the door.

'It is the will of God.' As far as Beloved was concerned, that was that; nobody disobeyed the will of God. Agnes was not so easily put off. What about her family? Should they not be consulted? If she were going to be married her family should know about it. Then there was the matter of the bridesmaids, the bottom drawer and the wedding gown. They would have to make arrangements, settlements.

'You will consider none of these things,' Prince commanded irritably. 'In this affair you must not think of the world, but of God.'

'My mother,' Agnes replied anxiously; 'she really ought to be told.'

'God is your father and your mother.'

Agnes, now thoroughly rattled, started to talk about lawyers. 'What on earth do you want a lawyer for, Dear?' Mrs Starky asked her in a surprised voice.

'For the little ones.'

'What little ones?'

'Children,' Agnes managed to get out. 'Our children ... the children of our marriage.'

Prince rose up. 'You will have no children,' he thundered. 'Your marriage with our brother will be spiritual only; your love to your husband will be pure, according to the will of God. Amen.'

Agnes left the room, confused, defeated and betrothed. The Holy Ghost had been more than a match for her; the will of God could not be challenged, at least not before breakfast. Later Agnes began to see that the will of God bore a remarkable resemblance to the will of Beloved. She also suspected that her bethrothal to brother Thomas was less of a gift to her from God than a gift to Beloved of the six thousand pounds of her inheritance. The exclusively spiritual nature of her marriage looked suspiciously like a ploy to prevent the arrival of legal progeny who might demand a share of the loot. Neither Beloved nor the Holy Ghost intended to share the spoils with outsiders. In due course Agnes was to fight back, and cross swords with the heavenly host—but by that time it was too late.

Later the same day Agnes's sisters, Harriet and Clara, went like lambs to the slaughter. They put up no resistance. Harriet was betrothed to Lewis Price, Clara to William Cobbe. Thus it came to pass that on that day a sum of no less than £18,000 was swept into the common fund, controlled entirely by H.J. Prince. The Father, the Son and the Holy Ghost rejoiced; it had been a profitable two hours.

The marriage ceremonies were solemnised, for some reason, at Swansea. Perhaps one of the Lampeter Brethren had a living there, or perhaps the Welsh were more tolerant of bizarre, spiritual-type weddings. It was certainly arranged and performed with indecent haste. The three prospective brides were allowed no time to reconsider, no time to go home to mother. The will of God did not allow them to communicate with any of their relatives or friends. They were kept incommunicado, advised to keep their mouths shut and do as they were told.

Prince made the necessary financial arrangements with remarkable speed, drawing everything together legally. For Agnes, the full implications of her impending fate had not sunk in entirely. She was sufficiently hypnotised to become partly reconciled to the betrothal, but being a woman, could not dismiss the sinful belief that marriages were mainly for the procreation of the species. She would have liked to retain some of her inheritance to that end. Prince had to speak to her strongly: such fleshly temptations were entirely against the will of God, the very suggestion of sexual consummation was heresy. 'Down on your knees woman!' he had ordered. 'Pray for your soul.' The small spirit of rebellion was quelled with threats of damnation, reduction to the ranks, exile to the pigsties. Agnes submitted—for the time being.

In view of what was to follow later, and the fact that Agnes was by no means unattractive, Prince may well have sugared the pill. He was shrewd enough to realise that Agnes was not entirely under his influence, nor was she the type of woman who could be entirely dominated by threats. And Prince was capable of using other means to the glory of God. Thomas, who was to be Agnes's future husband, was completely under the will of the Almighty, utterly dominated, successfully brainwashed. He obeyed the will of God without question and was celibate by command, and almost certainly remained so all his life. Prince was not, certainly not. Neither in the end was Agnes!

The couples were married without much ceremony. Starky gave all three of the brides away, going up and down the aisle like a shuttle. Prince watched in the shadows. None of the ladies had been able to communicate with family or friends. Their husbands were for the most part complete strangers, unlikely to share their beds, or even their rooms. None of the marriages would be consummated, at least not by the husbands. But nevertheless they were entirely legal: the contracts had been drawn up, the will of God obeyed.

A few days later Prince assembled the faithful into the unfinished church of the Agapemone at Spaxton. He gave thanks to God.

He had every reason to do so.

I am come into my garden, my sister, my spouse; I have gathered my myrrh with my spice; I have eaten my honeycomb with my honey; I have drunk my wine with my milk; eat, O friends; drink, yea, drink abundantly O Beloved.
Thus has the Son of Man manifested himself among us with eyes like a flame of fire.

Br. Thomas and Br. Starky
The Agapemone, 1862

Abduction by Night

Prince returned to Weymouth, leaving a substantial number of his 'saints', as Dixon called them, in makeshift accommodation within the grounds of the Agapemone. This was not a particularly wise move, but even he could not be in two places at once. Moreover he made the mistake of leaving Agnes Nottidge and George Thomas at Spaxton, and Agnes's devotion to the deity was crumbling.

Thomas was a weak man, easily dominated by stronger personalities. With Prince out of the way, Agnes began to realise that she had been conned. It was not so much the marriage she objected to, but the unnatural restrictions laid upon it. She craved for sexual fulfilment, and longed for the children which were to be denied her. The fruits of marriage, the very motive for its existence, consummation, procreation—all had been forbidden. It was a non-marriage, a sham, a legal chicanery engineered by Beloved to get his grasping hands on her money. Agnes boiled and set to work on her celibate husband.

Thomas probably rejected her sexual blandishments, for he was far more afraid of Prince than his wife. But he did succumb in some measure to her powerful invective. He listened to her, allowed her to influence him, to keep him away from Prince, even to disobey him upon occasion. This was not at all in order: Agnes was engendering mutiny. Beloved reached for the two-edged sword. It arrived by special messenger in the form of a curt note in the master's own hand. 'Brother Thomas,' the note thundered, 'I command you to arise, and come to Weymouth, Amen.'

Surprisingly, Thomas did not arise and go to Weymouth.

He went instead to Llandilo to visit his mother, at the insistence of Agnes. This was mutiny indeed, incurring the wrath of God. Orders were issued, emissaries sent to Llandilo with threats, entreaties, gentle persuasion and earnest prayer. Agnes could not withstand the full frontal assault of H.J. Prince and the Holy Ghost, and was forced to surrender without terms. The erring couple returned to Weymouth for trial and punishment.

The tribunal sat in the drawing room of the house in Belfield Terrace. The wretched Agnes was dragged before her sisters and their husbands, Price and Cobbe, who, together with Starky, Mrs Starky and Prince, set about her unmercifully. Thomas, it appears, was received more as an innocent victim than a culprit. The full force of divine indignation was directed at Agnes. The poor woman was blasted from all sides, her two sisters surpassing themselves in fury. When they had finished and Agnes was reduced to a snivelling, broken wreck, Prince strode in for the kill. 'If you dare attempt to influence your husband again,' he told her, 'in acting contrary to my commands, God will crush you out of the way.' Such was the power of the spirit, heavy as a hammer, sharper than a two-edged sword. Thomas was called in and made to declare his will. 'Agnes,' he stuttered, 'I command you to obey henceforth the spirit of God in me, made known to me through the servant of the Lord.' Agnes bowed her head and left the room weeping. The mutiny had been quelled and discipline restored—for the time being.

Prince, ever voracious when it came to money, was in hot pursuit of the fourth and youngest Nottidge girl, Louisa. She too was worth six thousand pounds, but somehow seems to have escaped her sisters' untimely fate. Prince was hopefully casting round for a suitable husband for her. Agnes got to hear about this and in one last gesture of defiance, wrote her sister a letter of warning.

The letter never arrived, for it never left Belfield Terrace. Prince, his own self-appointed censor, read all the mail; Agnes's letter fell into his hands. She felt the power of his displeasure.

That night she was confronted by Thomas as she was going to her room. 'You are lost,' he told her emotionally. 'You have crossed the Servant of the Lord.' The words her husband uttered, and the manner in which he uttered them, struck fear into Agnes. She must have guessed the reason, realised that Prince had opened and read her letter, and that punishment would follow. In that she was quite correct. They transferred her to a bare attic room, forbade her to see her husband ever again, and set her to work in the kitchen.

Prince, having once again restored discipline, left Weymouth to take up residence in Spaxton. The Agapemone was almost complete, the great wall erected, the gardens laid out. The Kingdom of Heaven was rising rapidly, and it was time to enter in.

But Agnes was not entirely finished. Prince, comfortably installed in the best rooms of the Agapemone, received an uncomfortable jolt by way of a gossiping servant. Agnes was pregnant! And the faithful had doubts as to who was the father.

Prince put on his finest performance. 'This comes,' he groaned, 'of sin. She is faithless, she is fallen; she must be cast away.'

Such was the rage of the Servant of the Lord, so furious the notes that rushed from Spaxton to Weymouth that not only Agnes, but her sisters as well, trembled for their fate. They too were under threat of being cast away, never to see their husbands again. The wrath of God was upon them. Everybody turned on Agnes, accusing her of ungodly behaviour, dissemination, lewd promiscuity. She was a whore, a prostitute, a fallen woman.

Probably the only existing photograph of H.J. Prince, this shows him in his dotage, supported by Smyth-Pigott and surrounded by the Heavenly Host. The shot was taken outside the Agapemone a few years before his death

Strangely, nobody accused Thomas of consummating his marriage or condemned him for exercising his conjugal rights. Agnes was expelled from the community. She went home to her mother at Rosehill and gave birth to a son, George. She never saw her husband again, or her money. But when the child was four years old, Starky attempted to kidnap him. He was repulsed and the whole matter taken to law. Nobody knows why Starky did this, since he was obviously not the boy's father, but then in all probability neither was Thomas.

Having disposed of the troublesome Agnes, Prince was free to set to work on her youngest sister. There would be no interference from Harriet or Clara, now thoroughly obedient to the will of God and well under control. As for Louisa, it would only be a question of time. Prince had already captured her soul; all that remained was her money. But Louisa, like Agnes, was to furrow the brow of the Servant of the Lord.

It was not that Louisa was disloyal or rebellious, God forbid. The youngest Nottidge girl was utterly devoted to her master in Christ, ready and eager to oblige him in every way; she and her inheritance were ripe for plucking. Prince reached out for the financial plum and had his hand bitten.

The remnants of the Nottidge family—two sons, one of them in holy orders—were by no means delighted at the prospect of seeing yet another six thousand pounds of their father's fortune falling into the grasping hands of the Holy Ghost. They were determined young men, sufficiently determined to resort to violence.

Prince, in his wisdom, had ordered Louisa into his presence at Spaxton, the better to work on her. Since the Agapemone was unfinished, the sacrificial victim had been lodged in a cottage in the grounds, under the beady eye of Mrs Prince. Edward Nottidge and the Reverend Pepys Nottidge, together with an accomplice, had followed their sister to her destination and were skulking about, ready to pounce.

One dark night, when the two ladies were alone and unguarded, the three conspirators forced their way into the cottage by the back door, burst into Louisa's bedroom and ordered her to pack up and leave. Louisa naturally resisted. Her brothers first tried gentle persuasion—their mother was ill and was asking for Louisa; she must hurry to her bedside before it was too late. Louisa refused to move. She did not in any case believe them and, if she had, it would not have made much difference. The servant of the Lord overruled filial obedience. She simply stood and screamed.

Mrs Prince, awakened by the shindig, fluttered up in her nightgown in time to see her charge bundled forcibly down the stairs out of the back door and into a waiting coach. The customers in the Lamb Inn, hearing Louisa's frantic screams, turned out to watch. It seems that nobody was prepared to go to the rescue of the unfortunate woman who was whisked off into the night.

As far as the spectators were concerned the drama had been an entertaining interlude. They watched the coach splashing away in the darkness and returned to their unfinished pints. But for Louisa it was the beginning of an unnerving experience.

The coach travelled through the night on its way to London. Louisa yelled, screamed and fought, doing her utmost to attract any would-be rescuers. But her brothers and their accomplice cunningly passed her off as a lunatic, and the more she struggled and yelled, the more credence she gave to their ploy. So successful did it become that, upon arriving in London, the unfortunate lady's relatives had no difficulty in having her incarcerated in a lunatic asylum.

With the apparently insane Louisa securely locked up in a madhouse, the Nottidge family had won the first round.

At least one portion of the family fortune had been saved. But the Nottidge family had overlooked the formidable powers of the Holy Ghost.

Prince, skulking in Spaxton, was not one to allow himself to be bested by mere mortals. He sent forth envoys to scour the country: Thomas, Cobbe, Starky and many of the faithful ventured in search of the flower so brutally torn from their midst. They had little success. The Nottidge family had taken care to keep Louisa's unpleasant prison so close a secret that not even Prince could find her. The Holy Ghost with all his divine power seemed confounded; or was he?

Like all good melodramas the story has a happy ending. Louisa, after about eighteen months under lock and key and, one would like to think, with the help of the Holy Ghost, managed to escape from the madhouse. She was undoubtedly a woman of spirit and determination, and it needed all that to escape from a Victorian lunatic asylum. But she did, and made her way to a small private hotel in Cavendish Square. Cobbe, still searching on the orders of Prince, discovered her whereabouts and arrived to escort her back to Spaxton. But both the Nottidge family and the madhouse officials were hot on the trail, and Louisa was picked up at Paddington station as she and Cobbe were about to board a train. The unfortunate lady was returned to the asylum and locked up once more.

But now Prince and the faithful knew where she was. They also knew that she was not mad; at least not all that mad. So Cobbe, who was Louisa's brother-in-law through his marriage to Clara, applied to the Commissioners of Lunacy for her release. An inquiry was held, and in spite of violent protestations from the Nottidge family, Louisa was pronounced sane.

The day after her release she went with Thomas to Prince's broker in London to transfer £5,728 of her inheritance to the account of Henry James Prince. *How wonderful are thy ways O Lord.* Two bloodhounds were purchased for the protection of the faithful.

Louisa lived happily ever after behind the walls of the Agapemone.

But the Nottidge family had the last word, for in 1860 when Louisa died and was put away in the garden with the other failed immortals, her will was contested.

The case of Nottidge v. Prince was held in the Vice-Chancellor's Court in June 1860. Prince himself gave evidence, but in spite of his divine intervention, the court held that the gift of £5,728 had been obtained under the influence of delusion and deception, 'by imposing a belief on the mind of a weak woman by the defendant that he sustained a supernatural character,' the judge declared. 'The stock must be transferred to the plaintive as legal personal representative of Miss Louisa Nottidge, and all the dividends which have accrued on it since her death paid to the plaintive. The defendant must pay to the plaintiff all the costs of the suit.'

The judge was condemned to ever-lasting perdition, but the Nottidge family got back its money.

The battle for Louisa's inheritance was one of many legal wrangles that plagued the Agapemone over the years. The son of God was never entirely scrupulous over financial matters; the Holy Ghost was above the law.

At the time of Louisa's kidnapping the Agapemone was nearing completion. In 1846 it was ready for occupation.

Prince collected his followers from Belfield Terrace and moved into the great house. It was a splendid place, the last word in luxury and comfort, a new heaven created by a new God, a palace fit for a king. Prince was a king fit for such a palace. He ruled over the faithful in undisputed divine sovereignty for fifty-three years, until, to the surprise of all concerned, he died in 1899.

The Agapemone, or Abode of Love as it was popularly known, did not just consist of one large house surrounded by a wall. The immediate area covered several acres, laid out with expensive lawns, shrubs and exotic plants. Cottages, stables and conservatories were clustered round the central building, the palace of the new Saviour, over which flew his personal standard. A farm and two hundred acres of prime Somerset pasture supplied its basic needs. A fluctuating population of between sixty and two hundred saints lived and worked, and kept their master in the style that he required as of divine right.

Prince ruled despotically, absolutely. Nobody, not even the servants, received a penny for their pains. Everybody from the Angel of the Seventh Seal down to the humblest chambermaid lived only to serve the Lamb of God, Beloved. The community was strictly segregated, the more attractive women, the selected ones, living with Prince in the main building. The less attractive women and the men were accommodated in cottages in the grounds, husbands living apart from their wives and everybody watching to make sure that no salacious contact was made between man and woman.

In spite of these restrictions there was no shortage of postulants. Whilst Starky, with his connexions in the county and amongst the aristocracy, remained with Prince, the establishment had a tenuous respectability. Indeed, for a time, Prince became fashionable. His sermons and pamphlets were widely read, and his dogmas were pondered over by earnest theologians. Well-to-do citizens paid large sums of money to gain admittance to the Agapemone. One London merchant is said to have paid over a thousand pounds for the privilege of serving Beloved as his liveried butler.

Prince, of course, enjoyed himself immensely. He ate well, drank well—he had left his total abstinence period far behind—and stocked his cellars with the best wines. Above all, he exercised absolute authority over a large number of men and women who worshipped him as God. Life was pleasant, heavenly perhaps, and some of the women were most desirable.

But what of his religious duties, his apostolic calling? These were strangely muted. No longer did the flesh revolt him. The austere evangelist of earlier days, the castigator of sinners, was becoming bland. There was no austerity for Beloved in the Agapemone, that was reserved for the faithful, the erring faithful. The church was decorated like a bar-parlour, complete with billiard table and periodicals. They sang hymns when it pleased them, played billiards when it pleased them, frequently ignoring the sabbath as just another day. It was a lazy dreamlike affair.

The old fires were never entirely quenched, however, never quite put out by the soft waters of good living. Prince knew very well that if he were to remain at the pinnacle he must dominate and exert his personality. This he did effectively, the two-edged sword always within reach, the wrath of God striking fear into the heart of any saint who crossed his path. There was only one God in the Abode of Love and Beloved was his name.

And to some extent the evangelism continued, at least for a while. Open-air meetings were held in Spaxton and Bridgwater, and trumpets blew to announce the Day of Judgement. The word of God was spread abroad even to London in those dog-days. But this was before the coming of the Great Manifestation, the day when Beloved selected a suitable virgin and took her flesh with the power and authority of the Holy Ghost.

The first thing that Jesus Christ did by this Spirit to redeem the earth was to create a new heaven.

Brother Prince
The Agapemone, August 15th, 1856

The Chosen

It is difficult to understand the motive behind the extraordinary aberration that led to the rape of Miss Paterson in the Church of the Agapemone. Prince had everything going for him, including power, money and the adoration of beautiful women.

His way of life was lordly. In 1851 he visited the Great Exhibition, driving through Hyde Park in an open carriage recently purchased from the Queen Mother. He had an equipage of enormous splendour, preceded by bareheaded outriders who proclaimed, 'He who cometh in the name of the Lord.' It caused a stir even amongst the blasé socialites of the capital. Passing horsemen were seen to glance enviously at the alluring beauties attending the Lamb of God. Prince was at the pinnacle of an extraordinary progress from rags to riches, from genteel penury to flamboyant opulence. Letters sent through the post addressed to, 'Our Lord God, Spaxton, Somerset', arrived frequently and without delay at the Agapemone. He was rich and famous; what more did he want?

Prince justified the ceremony in terms of his own twisted theology. This was set out in *The Little Book Open*, published in 1856 soon after the event. The book contains a great deal of mystical mumbo-jumbo, wild accounts of the Angel of the Lord descending on brother Prince with orders from above. 'This was the mighty angel that came down from heaven clothed with a cloud, even the Holy Ghost [Prince] in the new heaven He had formed. This was the bringing in of judgement, for Jesus Christ was in him, coming in a cloud.' The basic ideology that emerges from the quagmire is

Prince's old dogma of dispensation followed by judgement, followed by dispensation or a covenant with God. Jesus, according to Beloved, closed one dispensation and opened a new covenant by reconciling the spirit of man with God. He, Prince, was going to do exactly the same thing, only he was going to do it with the flesh. The enormous conceit of the man is breathtaking. He informs the world that he took the flesh, 'absolutely, in his own sovereign will, and with the power and authority of God.' Moreover he did not consult the flesh beforehand, or make known to it in any way his intentions. He had no respect for any other will than his own and was in no way influenced by what others would think or say. He took the flesh as it was—ignorant, indifferent, independent, at enmity against God, and having nothing to commend it to Him. But he took it in love.

Mrs Paterson, the widow with the pretty daughter who had joined the faithful at Weymouth, was dead. Death in the Agapemone was considered a sin, in fact, the ultimate sin. It probably stemmed from Prince's unsuccessful career as a doctor—anybody dying under his care being *ipso facto* a sinner. Anybody doing the same in the Agapemone, where death did not exist amongst true believers, had obviously failed. They were therefore put away in the garden without benefit of clergy. Mrs Paterson had suffered the same fate that in the end Prince himself was to suffer—although he managed to put it off for longer than most. She was buried in the garden amongst the tulips and exotic plants.

Her daughter had lived on with the faithful and, at the time of the Great Manifestation, had developed into a stunningly beautiful, nubile girl of sixteen. Prince quite obviously lusted after her, and may even have been genuinely in love with the girl. He was approaching middle-age, a time of life when young virgins not infrequently have a strong appeal, and there is no doubt that Prince desired the young lady.

He could have taken her, had he wished, in almost any circumstances. A little extra religious instruction behind the conservatory, for instance, or a few prayers at bed-time might have passed unchallenged.

But no—Prince was divine, the visible manifestation of God on earth. A furtive snatching of Miss Paterson's maidenhead in uncomfortable circumstances was not fitting for the servant of the Lord. Prince consulted the Holy Ghost.

Victorian men appear to have been obsessed by virginity. Deflowering virgins was one of the principal fantasies of mid-nineteenth-century gentlemen. Most enterprising brothels provided unsullied young girls from the age of twelve upwards. These could be raped for as little as ten guineas. Less opulent clients might, for a small fee, witness the performance and listen to the screams of the victim through discreet apertures in the walls of the brothel bedroom. It was a popular pastime, as popular as flagellation. There is no evidence that Prince indulged in the latter, but he certainly indulged in the former, in a most spectacular manner.

Prince had called upon the Holy Ghost for advice. The deity was not required to assist at the actual ceremony—Prince knew exactly how that was to go—but it was necessary to justify it. It was a mere formality. The Holy Ghost justified Prince's eccentricities with formidable ease.

Beloved had progressed in many ways. The earnest, pious, penniless young man of Guy's Hospital and Lampeter was transformed into the undisputed spiritual head of a rich and devoted following. But he was a Victorian, had been ordained into the Church of England and had marinated in puritanical christian doctrine. He therefore needed to justify his sexual deviations as extravagantly, perhaps more extravagantly, than his religious deviations. Having done that, he could proceed without trouble to take what he wanted openly, with due ceremony, as his undisputed right. It was an attractive prospect, and he could do it. He could ravish this virgin, strip her naked, rape her in the name of God, and nobody—but nobody—could stop him.

The Holy Ghost did not delay. 'THE DAY OF JUDGEMENT HAS COME', Prince proclaimed to the faithful. God was about to extend His love from heaven to earth, from spirit to flesh, from soul to body. A virgin must be found, suitable to become the Bride of the Lamb. The Holy Ghost was to take the flesh of a virgin, to measure the temple of God; and the reed like unto a rod wherewith he would measure it, would be the flesh he was about to take.

The faithful, punch-drunk from frequent omnipotent commands, may not have understood the implication of what was to follow. Orders from above arrived with confusing rapidity and, like acts of parliament, required dogged unravelling. The saints were entitled to be confused. But on this occasion the meaning of the act was made abundantly clear. For Prince went on to advise the virgins—all the virgins—to prepare themselves. One of them, he announced, would be the 'Favoured One', the rod by which he would measure the temple of God. Even the dimmest virgin could hardly fail to realise that one of her number was about to suffer, 'a fate worse than death'—or a 'divine purification', which amounted to the same thing!

In the circumstances one might have expected a sudden exodus of nervous virgins leaping the walls of the Agapemone to escape the attentions of the Almighty. Choosing death before dishonour, they might dash themselves from the unfinished tower of the church. After all this was 1856, the peak of Victorian morality. There is no evidence of any such thing. The regulars in the Lamb Inn, always the first to notice and record the smallest signs of saintly agitation, appear to have quaffed on undisturbed. Not one virgin escaped, or apparently wanted to escape. Instead, with fluttering hearts and quivering bosoms, they prepared to meet their fate.

There is something of a pagan orgy about the Great Manifestation, as it was known within the Agapemone. It was a ritual sacrifice, the ravishing of a young girl upon the altar of the High Priest. But the only *recorded* description of what happened that day in the church of the Agapemone comes second-hand from Hepworth Dixon, picking up crumbs of information from his visit in 1867. By far the most detailed account, but this only by implication, comes from Prince himself. Judging from the contents of *The Little Book Open*, and a later more detailed justification, *The Counsel of God In Judgement*, the ceremony was, to say the least, startling.

Prince had no intention of spoiling the fun by announcing his choice beforehand. He was going to keep the virgins in cruel suspense, to prepare them for sacrifice. This was to be the Day of Judgement, the most sacred ceremony that the Agapemone, or indeed the world, had known. The flesh was to be purified, cleansed from filth, delivered from the lusts which defiled it. It would be taken as it was, because it pleased him to do so, pleased him to take this one lump of clay—dust of the ground, living earth, flesh—and make it new, according to his will and pleasure. All this, he declared, was to enable the faithful to see the character and mind of God manifested towards flesh.

The obsessive use of the word 'flesh' appears again and again in all Prince's writings. He reviles it, castigates it, wants it. One suspects that the Great Manifestation is the realisation of a fantasy that the evil flesh has no goodness and must be punished, taken. Miss Paterson must be raped, he convinced himself, not because she is desirable and he loves her, but because she is flesh, ignorant, indifferent, independent, at enmity against God. Reading between the lines of that last sentence which appears in *The Little Book Open*, it may

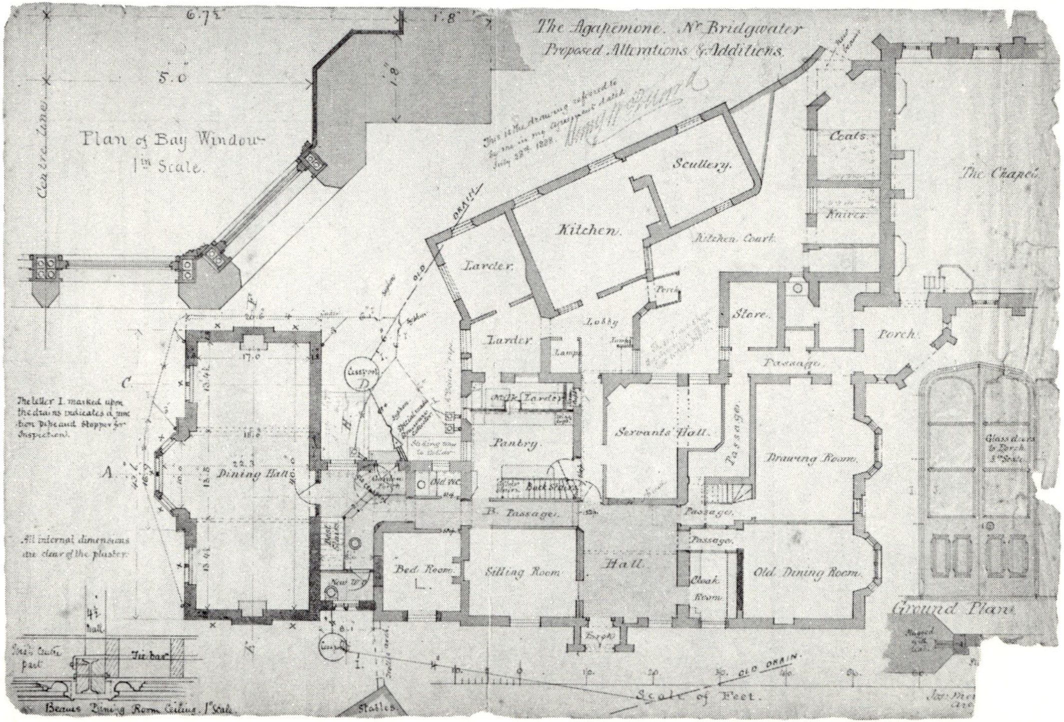

This plan, drawn up when alterations were proposed to the Agapemone in 1888, shows the ground floor of the main building and part of the chapel. Later plans indicate that upstairs there were sixteen bedrooms

Artist's impression of the Agapemone in 1850, showing Prince's equipage and the infamous bloodhounds. The artist has been careful to include Prince's personal device of a lion on the roof of the chapel, to the foreground

The Agapemone was shielded by high walls and solid gates

On the ground floor to the left of the door was the old dining room; to the right was the drawing room

The porch in the centre of this photograph (c. 1910) linked the main house with the chapel to the right

The large dining hall was on the ground floor to the rear of the house

A number of terraced cottages flanked the main house and chapel

just be that Miss Paterson had rejected Prince's advances, may even have teased him or laughed at him. In which case he would very likely have called upon the Holy Ghost to bring her to heel. It may just be that Prince devised the whole ceremony out of frustration and fury at being rejected. Such a rejection would have been new to the Lamb of God. He would have reached for the two-edged sword.

Whatever the motive, the outcome was the public defilement of a young girl in what was called a church.

It is impossible to describe the ceremony without a good deal of surmise and speculation. The faithful were assembled, the virgins arranged in white garments before the altar. The organ played hymns and the congregation sang. The atmosphere must have been nervous, to put it mildly. Nobody knew who was to be 'favoured', nobody quite knew what was going to happen or how it was to be done. The virgins had come like lambs to the slaughter; among them Miss Paterson. Perhaps in her innocence she had thought it a game; perhaps none of them believed it was about to happen. Perhaps some of them hoped it would. Nobody had tried to escape; they were all there in white, waiting to be ravished by the son of God.

Prince, preceded by Maber, who had been installed as the Angel of the Last Trumpet, entered in full canonicals accompanied by his retinue. The organ music sank to a murmur, the virgins trembled in their white frocks. The Lamb of God passed amongst them, slowly, arrogantly, as though examining stock at a market. He must have savoured every second of the preliminaries, revelling in the fluttering flesh and the heaving bosoms, until at last he stood before the indifferent, independent, delectable Miss Paterson.

Prince appears to have mastered her completely, for she behaved like a hypnotised rabbit. There was no independence now, no enmity, just submission on the couch before the altar in front of the congregation. The Lamb of God, full of glory, triumphantly removed Miss Paterson's frock—and her maidenhead—to the music of the organ and the singing of hymns.

'Thus the Holy Ghost took flesh in the presence of those whom he had called as flesh.' And the flesh submitted to the ordeal like an obedient child. Having completed the ceremony, Prince rose up to announce that flesh was now free from sin and was one with the Holy Ghost; the faithful could now rejoice. So saying, he departed followed by his retinue and a tearful Miss Paterson with her head bowed. We do not know if Miss Paterson enjoyed her part in the ceremony, but she certainly never rejected Prince again. Perhaps she had not rejected him in the first place. Who knows?

As for the faithful—they had mixed feelings. Sister Ellen, talking to Dixon in the Agapemone, recalls her memories of that day as, 'a very tender and solemn time, the most tender and solemn time we have ever known. I have never felt so strange a joy and wonder as I felt in that hour.' Julia, Prince's wife, was present during the ceremony and raised no objection. Her brother Samuel Starky was adamant: 'I know that what was done was right and holy in the Lord,' he told Dixon. 'You must be sure that I am quite sincere in my belief, for my salvation rests upon the truth of what I say.'

But not everybody was enthusiastic. One or two of the weaker brethren were heard to murmur that the Holy Ghost had gone too far, that it was not the sort of thing you did in church. If this were the way God carried on in his house on earth, how would he behave aloft? Several people, Lewis Price included, became anxious.

Prince felt obliged to explain the meaning of the ceremony once more. In the ordinary way he would not have bothered, but some waverers were threatening to leave and—worse—

take their money with them. Unfortunately he appears to have been so convinced of his own spirituality that he felt able to tell the faithful that the affair was entirely out of this world. It was not Prince who took Miss Paterson in the church, but the Holy Ghost; it was a divine union. He had always said that anyway, but this time he rammed it home, assuring them that, because of the union, Miss Paterson was sinless and incapable of committing sin. In other words he implied that if the faithful cared to hang on they would see for themselves that this was so, since there would be no progeny. He could not have made a bigger mistake.

Miss Paterson, in spite of her purity, was in due time seen to be pregnant. This appears to have surprised Prince every bit as much as it surprised the faithful. 'You would have wept tears of blood for him,' Sister Ellen agonises to Dixon, 'if you had seen how much he suffered; he who feels so keenly, and who has to bear the burden of us all.' Beloved's suffering was understandable; his bread and butter was flitting furtively away into the night. He was losing cash, and something had to be done. Prince, as usual, consulted the Holy Ghost.

The 'communiqué' issued to stem the tide is described in the first chapter of this book. It put the blame for the mishap conveniently upon the devil who had somehow managed to impregnate Miss Paterson, whilst Prince and the Holy Ghost were not looking. The approaching confinement was the devil's work, the child his progeny. Beloved had nothing to do with it. It was neither terribly convincing nor very kind to the child. To be born of the devil can be a disadvantage in most circumstances; in the Agapemone, amongst the Heavenly Host, it must have been particularly trying.

Nevertheless, the 'Final Dispensation', as Prince called it, worked well enough. With its help he was able to maintain his command of the situation and Miss Paterson continued to be unsullied. The torrent of fleeing faithful was reduced to a trickle.

But Prince had taken a battering. Whilst the Great Manifestation had merely shaken the faithful, its embarrassing result was near catastrophe. Many left, including the Reverend Lewis Price, one of Prince's original Lampeter Brethren and a devoted disciple. He escaped into the night, abandoning his wife in his haste and confusion. Beloved hung on to her firmly, for although Lewis Price was no particular loss, Harriet Price would be—she possessed an inheritance of six thousand pounds. When Price returned to claim her, Beloved, in the best tradition of medieval siege warfare, refused to give her up. Price took lodgings in the Lamb Inn and, to the vast entertainment of the regulars, made several hazardous attempts to rescue the incarcerated lady. The bloodhounds, however, proved altogether too much for him and he was forced to retire, bloody and bitten. Harriet eventually made her own escape and the drama had a happy ending—except for Beloved who lost two saints and six thousand pounds.

'Price's going,' Starky informed Dixon, 'was a sore trial to us, for he left the Abode in a very bad spirit.' It was indeed a heavy loss.

> This one man, myself, has Jesus Christ selected and appointed His witness to His counsel and purpose, to conclude the day of grace and to introduce the day of judgement, to close the dispensation of the spirit and to enter into covenant with the FLESH.

'The Little Book Open'—the testimony of Brother Prince, Voice the Fourth January 1857

The Ageing Beloved

When Dixon visited the Agapemone in 1867 the faithful had dwindled to some sixty souls. In the glorious days before the Great Manifestation and the disastrous Final Dispensation, there had been over two hundred saints at the Abode of Love. The wealth of the establishment was vast, amounting to hundreds of thousands of pounds according to some accounts. The saints, whatever they may have had to put up with from their eccentric deity, never suffered penury. The best that money could provide was at hand. True, the real luxury, the greatest comfort, the power and the glory belonged to Beloved, as was his due. Beloved was divine—as was Miss Paterson, come to that, in spite of the devil's successful and immoral attentions. Neither the Lamb or the bride of the Lamb was capable of sin.

The faithful—providing they behaved themselves, did exactly what they were told and supplied the Agapemone with ample funds—were also incapable of sin. Well almost, for this depended largely upon the whim of the Almighty, who could cancel the dispensation whenever the mood or necessity took him.

The more opulent faithful were free to do absolutely nothing, except wait about for Armageddon. The less opulent had to work, serving as chambermaids, stable-hands, gardeners, kitchen workers. They received no wages, but worked for love. Some of the chambermaids also made love for love, but only, of course, in a 'spiritual' way with the Lamb of God. There is at least one family living in Bridgwater today who descend from one of these spiritual unions, made in 1877 when Prince was sixty-six and still sexually strong.

An article in the *Illustrated London News* for March 29th, 1851, provides a wealth of information concerning the activities of the faithful in the Agapemone. One suspects that it is largely speculative, possibly influenced by the obliging regulars in the Lamb Inn. Nevertheless it is worth recording, if only as an example of the social history of the period.

The writer describes the situation of the Agapemone as, 'a gentle eminence, backed by the Quantock Hills, the area of the whole place enclosed being more than an acre.' He puts the number of residents at about sixty, some married, others unmarried. He informs us that there were children in the Agapemone, but in the phraseology of the brethren the term seems to mean the unmarried, the youngest 'child' being described as about twenty-four, the oldest forty!

Whoever gave the writer this information, either did not know of, or wished to ignore, the presence of Miss Paterson. He refers to the faithful as 'The Family', whilst Prince was referred to as 'God Incarnate', or 'God the Father', which is only a short step from the 'Godfather'. The writer continues, 'all the members of the Family appear to be persons of substance, though some of them have acquired their property by marriage. They live at their ease in much enjoyment, and rather mock at solemn professional men for their seriousness and their care. They profess merriment. They ride for pleasure, they hunt, they play at various games, and delight in hockey, especially on Sunday.'

Surely the hockey story must have come straight from the Lamb. One needs a good deal of imagination to picture teams of unfrocked clerics and portly archangels charging about brandishing hockey sticks—even on a Sunday. Billiards perhaps—but hockey?

'They have purchased a farm, but it does not appear that they cultivate the land themselves. Their property is managed in common by their chiefs, they take their meals in common, and have their pursuits in common. Their creed is typified by their practices. They have converted the chapel into a banqueting-house, and substitute feasting and enjoyment for privation and prayer. "If God be not life, happiness, and love," said one member of the Family, "then we do not know what God is." Every family, the same jolly fellow declared, should be an Agapemone.'

It sounds very 'jolly' indeed, this feasting and frolicking and playing hockey on Sundays. But it was not all fun and games. Beloved had his whimsical moments: 'latterly, it is said, a stricter kind of discipline has been introduced into the Family, and its chief thinks it right to enforce some kind of sumptuary regulation on the children. The ladies have been obliged, it is said, to lay aside caps, and cut off their hair, which is to be kept close shorn. The men, too, are treated like Russians, and, contrary to most other sects, which encourage growth of hair, they are ordered to shave close, annihilating whiskers and all, and keeping their heads like those of charity boys. It is said, too, that one of the children of the Family having taken lessons in love beyond the walls, was seized by force and carried back to the Agapemone. Not liking his treatment, he made his escape and has since carried pistols, according to report, to protect himself from the love of his friends.'

So much for the secular activities of the Family and their 'Godfather'. What of their religious activities? The Agapemone was, after all, a community of saints, in covenant with God, passing from one dispensation to another.

'You hold,' Dixon asked the Lamb of God in the Agapemone, 'that the day of Grace is past?'

'We know,' Prince answered in his wisdom, 'that the day of grace is past; that Christ has left the mercy-seat; and that the day of judgement is at hand.'

'You expect the world to pass away?'

'The world is no more,' Prince answered, without batting an eyelid. 'God has withdrawn from it His own.'

'Do you, then, hold that all mankind beyond these walls—the millions after millions of men and women, will all be lost?'

'It is God's will; not ours. Has it not always been so? How many were sheltered in the ark? Was any man called save Abraham and his seed? How many men did Jesus draw aside unto Himself?'

There was no answer to that; Dixon was forced to change the subject; Prince was nodding off to sleep.

'What have you done since the day of judgement?' Dixon asked Starky after Prince had finally nodded off.

'Not much,' he answered with blinding honesty; 'at least, not much that you would consider work. We have sent through the foreign ambassadors a letter, each in his own tongue, to the kings and peoples of the earth, making known to all men that flesh is saved from death. If men will not hear us, what are we to do?'

'You teach?'

'No.'

'Preach?'

'No.'

'Write?'

'No.'

'Read?'

'Not much?'

'Farm?'

'No.'

'Feed the poor?'

'No.'

'Send out missions?'

'No.'

'How do you pass the time?' Dixon asked despairingly.

'We have no time.'

'You rise at dawn, you sleep at dark; how do you enjoy the intervals?' he ventured.

'We eat and drink,' came the emphatic answer, and then almost as an afterthought: 'we wait on God. It is not for us to force his steps. In his own time the end will come.'

'They renounce prayer' says the article in the *Illustrated London News*; 'they sing the praises of the Lord sometimes in the open air, and sometimes in unintelligible gibberish. They act as their feelings prompt them.' So much for religious activity. There was not, it appears, all that much that the faithful could do, except sit tight, put their trust in Beloved and wait hopefully for the next dispensation.

From Starky's conversation with Dixon, the reader might assume that Prince had lost some of his ascetic, evangelistic zeal. Certainly he had progressed backwards in terms of self-denial. The gaunt young zealot of Lampeter, who had dashed the sherry glass from the hand of the Vice-Principal was crucified, dead and buried. The spirit that had risen on the third day was something of a gourmet and, like the Reverend Alfred Ollivant, certainly knew the difference between port wine and claret. Divinity had mellowed Prince, but it had not debilitated him. The two-edged sword was always handy and often used.

Following the Great Manifestation, Miss Paterson was raised to glory. She became the first bride of the Lamb, the undefiled one. She would not be the last! In due course Prince wrote a sort of gospel, a manifesto, in which he laid down rules and duties for the instruction of brides of the Lamb: 'She does not live to do her own will, or to please herself, but to do His will, and to please Him. She daily delivers herself up to Him, and lays down her whole life in soul and body on the altar of His dear name.'

Strangely, the women revelled in it. None of them appear

to have raised any objections, least of all Julia, Prince's wife, who seems to have enjoyed the ceremony and its aftermath as much as anybody. In 1896 when Prince extended his ministry to London, a church was built at Clapton. The principle motif on the stained-glass windows was a lurid depiction of the submission of womankind to man. Prince's views on the status of women were Oriental, to say the least. Yet there was never any shortage of them in the Agapemone. To be fair, his views on the status of both sexes, compared to his own superiority, were impartially condescending.

Dixon was convinced that the beautiful saints who were draped about Beloved in the room furnished like a lady's boudoir, made up a seraglio. He was also convinced, although never able to prove, that the gorgeous sister Zoe was, in fact, Miss Paterson. She was the right age, and her behaviour seemed to confirm his own romantic notions about the victim of Prince's sexual aberration. How long she remained in favour we do not know. If Dixon were right in his surmise, Miss Paterson was still firmly in the driving seat some eleven years after the event. Prince informed the world in *The Little Book Open* that he kept the flesh with Him continually by day and by night, took it wherever He went, was not ashamed of it, and made its life agreeable by affording to it the enjoyment of every simple and innocent gratification. The beautiful sister Zoe certainly fitted the description of favoured flesh, certainly gave Dixon the impression of one who was enjoying simple and innocent gratification to the full. But was she Miss Paterson? Alas, we shall never know.

It is quite possible that Miss Paterson remained the number one bride for many years, for her youth and beauty as well as her obvious devotion probably ensured her position. Prince was undoubtedly enamoured, and never, for instance, publicly castigated her for allowing the devil to have his way. She remained unsullied in spite of producing Satan's progeny, which was a remarkable achievement. Prince undoubtedly adored the flesh, Miss Paterson's flesh especially. The ceremony was created, one suspects, out of hot desire, coupled with something amounting to love.

Prince may have loved Miss Paterson, but he was very much influenced by, indeed had assumed the mantle of, the Holy Ghost. And that spirit, having tasted flesh, was ready to sanctify further suitable virgins, or any attractive woman in need of spiritual uplift. There was nothing to stop him. It seems likely that Prince had indulged before, not with the first or even the second Mrs Prince—although he may have favoured both—but with Agnes Nottidge, during her rebellious period, and possibly numerous other ladies.

Prince was quite capable of seducing the pious women who flocked to his meetings, but it had to take place discreetly behind locked doors. It was a hazardous, hasty, neurotic purification. The Great Manifestation, however, made it all so much easier. From then on Prince could indulge himself openly, and ascribe it to the Holy Ghost:

> Here is the land of pure delight;
> Here dawns the day that knows no night;
> Here where I walk with Him in white;
> Here, here, here, rejoice!
> *(The Voice of the Bride—Hymn No. 16)*

Beloved, having procured the divine right of flesh-taking, had now to turn his attention to rather more mundane matters. The faithful were still wavering, and a small number were escaping. Cries of enraged sinners, unreasonably shocked by rumours of the Great Manifestation, could be heard without. Victorian moralists, in a frenzy of outraged righteousness, were screaming abuse and demanding retribution. Beloved was insulted by clergymen, publicans and sinners alike. Crowds descended upon Spaxton to yell abuse, consume flagons of scrumpy in the Lamb Inn, and hopefully to catch a brief glimpse of a fleeting saint.

The more determined moralists tried to invoke an ancient Georgian act of parliament, whereby a citizen could be prosecuted for holding a public ceremony in a private place. This was immediately shot down by Prince, who knew the law as well as anybody, and declared that the ceremony had been anything but public. If he had intended it to be public, then he would have thrown the Agapemone open to the world and sent out invitations. They could not get him on that issue. In fact they could not get him at all. Only the faithful could do that.

The clamour set up by the outside world did penetrate the walls of the Agapemone, causing some of the saints to wonder if the Ark of the Covenant was sinking in a sea of perishing sinners. And it did encourage a small number to reach for their lifebelts and swim for it.

But it was not the prime cause of the panic that had set in. That was quite different.

The ceremony in the church had been heralded as the coming of a new dawn. By taking flesh, the Holy Ghost would save the world and introduce a new heaven and a new earth. The next dispensation, for which the saints had been waiting patiently, was to start with the purification of Miss Paterson. Prince in his desire for the virgin was prepared to offer almost anything by way of justification for the fell deed. Indeed as far as he was concerned, there was no doubt the taking of Miss Paterson's virginity would be paradise enough. The rending asunder of tiresome social strictures, the freedom to indulge in unlimited future intercourse, would amount to a new heaven and a new earth.

But the faithful, since they were not encouraged to follow their leader's example and leap upon the nearest virgin, and were probably not inclined to do so anyway, could find little sign of a change for the better in the world about them. It appeared alarmingly similar to the old world. Heavenly choirs were not noticeably discovered singing anthems in the sunset. Chariots of fire were not arriving to offer free transport to glory. Nothing had changed—except the pregnant Miss Paterson.

The less committed faithful, such as the Reverend Lewis Price, began to nod their heads in doubt. So when the distant bellows of outraged moralists filtered through the protecting walls of the Agapemone, and Miss Paterson was finally brought to bed with a fine bouncing girl, they cracked completely, packed their bags and fled.

Beloved, after due consultation with the Holy Ghost, brought out a series of pamphlets entitled—*The Little Book Open; The Testimony of Br. Prince Concerning what Jesus Christ had Done by His Spirit to Redeem the Earth; In Voices from Heaven.* It was not an apologia, nor was it altogether a justification. It simply stated a number of incontrovertible facts. The Holy Ghost had taken flesh in his own right with the power and authority of God, and by so doing He had redeemed the world. Anybody foolish enough to challenge that, coming as it did from heaven, was no less than a sinner bound for damnation.

The pamphlets drove the outside world into paroxysms of rage and made moralists hysterical. The pamphlets were bound into a single volume and sold briskly. Although they were not intended for the outside world, Prince could never resist offers from publishers or money in any form. Their primary object was to placate the faithful and bring them to heel. As such, they worked admirably. Prince was able to retain such devoted and affluent disciples as Samuel Starky as well as Hotham Maber, of the Last Trumpet, the Seventh Seal and ten thousand pounds. Unfortunately a number had already escaped, and Prince's final pamphlet, the *Fifth*

Voice from Heaven, was less than convincing. This was the one that blamed the devil for Miss Paterson's interesting condition, but even the faithful found it dubious. Prince was obliged to call in existing copies from the printer, burn the rest and thereafter maintain a discreet and mysterious silence.

Beloved was now faced with further trials and tribulations. The case of Nottidge v. Prince has already been mentioned. It took place in 1860, a few years after the Great Manifestation and concerned the inheritance of the youngest Nottidge girl, Louisa. Prince considered the inheritance his by divine right; the Nottidge family disagreed.

The case was sufficiently celebrated to be recorded in the *Law Reports* for the period. Whilst it resulted in defeat for the Lamb of God, it does illustrate the energy and determination which he displayed when defending his financial interests. It also supplies us with useful information as to the condition of the Agapemone after the Great Manifestation; the institution appears to be far from threadbare.

Mr Bacon Q.C., for the defendant, describes the Abode of Love as a large mansion house, with extensive gardens, conservatories, hothouses, pleasure-grounds and a farm. He informs the court that the residents enjoy every kind of comfort, including numerous horses of great value, both for riding and driving. They occasionally ride out in a carriage drawn by four horses.

On this evidence the Agapemone does not appear to have declined noticeably, or to have been greatly affected by departing faithful and the cries of moralists.

Another snippet of information recorded in the *Law Report* was that Beloved claimed to feed and clothe many poor in the neighbourhood. This was certainly true, and it is much to the credit of the Agapemone that this tradition was carried on to the end.

"THE LITTLE BOOK OPEN."

THE TESTIMONY

OF

BR. PRINCE

CONCERNING WHAT

JESUS CHRIST HAS DONE BY HIS SPIRIT

TO

REDEEM THE EARTH.

IN VOICES FROM HEAVEN.

VOICE THE FIRST.

LONDON:

C. A. BARTLETT, PATERNOSTER ROW;

BRIDGWATER: F. G. DOWTY, FORE-STREET.

1856.

PRICE ONE PENNY.

The title page of *The Little Book Open*, which contained Prince's remarkable justification for taking the flesh of a virgin in order to redeem the earth

In spite of his good works, Beloved lost the case and received a sample of somebody else's two-edged sword. The judge declared that his conduct was disgraceful, that he imposed his will on weak women by falsely and blasphemously pretending that he had a direct and divine mission. Beloved's reply is not recorded in the *Law Report*! Nevertheless he was able to inform the judge and the court, 'that the Holy Ghost by me did close the day of grace and introduce the judgement'. Which must have caused a few raised eyebrows.

The fortunes of the faithful fluctuated as Beloved emerged from his new heaven to fight bloody battles with legal gentlemen who rushed upon him in large numbers, demanding their clients' money back. The sinners in the Lamb Inn watched the comings and goings with interest. They augmented their entertainment by generating extravagant rumours of enormous orgies, mass love-ins, Saturnalian deviations, and anything else they could imagine might be happening behind the walls of the Agapemone. This drove the moralists into further convulsions and brought crowds rushing up from Bridgwater, providing more entertainment and exceeding profit for the Lamb Inn. The fact that the rumours were entirely without substance made little difference. Nobody would ever know what actually went on behind the high walls because nobody could get in. If they tried, 'the bloodhounds would get them', and that was always good for a laugh.

Prince, between bouts of litigation, wisely concentrated on securing the remaining faithful. To this end he generously promoted them into Angels and Archangels, Keepers of this, Keepers of that, Anointed Ones, Selected Ones, Undefiled Ones, Brothers and Sisters, brides of the Lamb. Witnesses were appointed to follow Maber about with his trumpet, to announce loudly, frequently and monotonously that, 'God has brought forth Beloved to be the Glory of Jesus Christ on earth.' It was a little pretentious but it occupied the faithful, reminding them who was the boss, and keeping them from wondering about the final dispensation and why it had not changed the world.

By 1867 things had settled into a kind of routine. The moralists had exhausted themselves. Only Dixon was interested enough to find his way through the closed doors and record the curious habits of the sect for posterity. The customers in the Lamb Inn had run out of imagination. The villagers began to accept the Agapemone and take pride in it in a curious way. It was, after all, unique.

The years passed, Beloved grew older, which was disturbing because he was immortal. But then Job lived for a number of years and he was not in the same league as Beloved when it came to divinity. Beloved might seem to be suffering the ravages of time, might have slowed down a little, might have withdrawn from the more tedious affairs of the Agapemone, but he was still capable of showing a lively interest in the younger female postulants, could still wield the two-edged sword, beat down the sinners, quell the doubtful. No, he would not die. Beloved was immortal, Beloved would live forever, of that there was no doubt.

As the years passed, the Son of God showed every sign of immortality. He outlived most of his contemporaries, who sinfully 'gave up the ghost' and were put away in the garden. He produced endless tracts and pamphlets, published his journals, composed a major religious manifesto, wrote enormous poems, numerous hymns, and busied himself with the spiritual affairs of the young ladies who, in spite of stern warnings from wrathful parents and parish parsons, came from near and far to bathe themselves in his divine presence. He never seems to have lost his charisma, and was never challenged. There is no evidence of any palace rebellions. The saints were content to obey and worship, content to potter about, placing their lives, their all, into the ever-open hands of H.J.Prince.

The grip slackened towards the end. Beloved, probably reluctantly, for he liked nothing more than complete command, was obliged to hand over the business affairs of the Agapemone to younger men. He certainly never, for one moment, relinquished his position of absolute authority, never allowed any of the younger men the slightest nibble at his cherry. Male saints lived in cottages in the garden, chaste, segregated, well out of range of temptation. There would be no lesser manifestations—brides of the Lamb were sanctified by the Holy Ghost, by the Holy Ghost alone. Beloved, approaching senility, was still a formidable guardian of morals—other people's morals.

The Agapemone drifted on into the 1890s. Most of the original Lampeter Brethren were dead, but the Almighty lived on. He was senile perhaps, but the saints rejoiced that he was immortal. Nobody contemplated the heretical thought that Beloved might die. Nobody—except one young man: the Reverend John Hugh Smyth-Pigott.

Take ye heed, watch and pray; for ye know not when the time is. Watch ye therefore, lest coming suddenly He find you sleeping. And what I say unto you I say unto all, Watch. *(Mark XIII. 32–37)*

Beloved, at this time, and under the circumstances in which you are now living, you will do well indeed to give constant and practical attention to this admonition.

Brother Prince
The Agapemone, 1887

A Second Messiah

The Reverend Smyth-Pigott was an ambitious man. He had many of Prince's attributes but little of his style. He was born of well-to-do parents, and seemed to have suffered, like many modern youths, from the generation gap. So much so that in the best tradition of Victorian romance he had run away to sea at an early age and had served before the mast as an ordinary seaman in the Merchant Navy. The open-air life had not agreed with him, being far too stark, dangerous and uncomfortable. He disliked the life, his shipmates and his officers—and they, without exception, disliked him. Moreover he was 'God-bothered', and no fun in the fo'c'sle. He did not last long in the Merchant Navy. Like Arthur Rees he turned to the Church, entered the London College of Divinity and was eventually ordained into the Church of England.

Not a great deal is known about Smyth-Pigott's early life. He was in many ways like Prince, in many ways different—completely different. He shared Prince's fascination for women, his ability to use the two-edged sword, his evangelic zeal, his fanaticism. He was capable of charm when it suited him, was endowed with astute business acumen and endless cunning. Life in the Merchant Navy had broadened his outlook, and he could tolerate, even charm, sinners when necessary, as well as condemn them. Prince was capable only of the latter. Smyth-Pigott was also more coldly ruthless than Prince. In many ways he was more formidable, and infinitely more dangerous.

Pigott, who had learned his rhetoric at the street corner, was a soap-box preacher in the Salvation Army, a saver of souls and fallen women. Much of his work as a salvationist was amongst the West End prostitutes, whom he brought passionately to God.

In 1882 he left the Salvation Army for a more lucrative appointment as curate of St Jude's parish church, Mildmay Park, London. He seems to have been a smash-hit with the young ladies of the parish who lapped up his powerful sermons, full of hidden innuendoes and sexual connotations. They discovered that churchgoing was fun, altogether different from the long rambling services and boring platitudes of the Vicar. They flocked round Smyth-Pigott in twittering coveys, flaunting their plumage, begging to be brought to God. Pigott set about them with a will! His sermons became more and more questionable, more and more daring. Before long, like Prince, he was usurping the throne of heaven. Like Prince he was admonished, asked to take his services elsewhere, and, like Prince, he flounced off altogether.

The first recorded mention of Pigott concerning himself with the Agapemone is in a letter written by Beloved to his London flock in 1889. After going on in his usual manner about 'the bowels of Jesus Christ', and his desire to be 'in the midst of my loved ones in London and elsewhere, to refresh them by my presence', he recommends Mr Pigott, 'whom the Lord in His loving kindness has appointed to be your pastor and guide.'

It is very unlikely that Prince would appoint someone to such an influential position outside the Agapemone unless he felt he could trust him completely. Smyth-Pigott was an opportunist, who must have heard about the Agapemone and, upon losing his living at St Jude's, gone down to Spaxton as a sympathiser in order to inspect the lay-out. He may have genuinely believed in Prince's divinity, although this is doubtful. It is far more likely that the young man had his eyes on the pickings, and realised that, if he played his cards accordingly, he might possibly inherit the kingdom after the demise of the Almighty.

Whatever happened before 1899, Pigott certainly came to the throne in 1902, and already in 1898 he was reported to be in charge of the Church of the Ark of the Covenant, which Prince and the faithful had built at Clapton. Pigott, in fact, wooed Prince and used his charm to worm his way into the old man's favour. He knew very well that Beloved was not immortal. He must have been the only person in the Agapemone, including Prince himself, who did.

In 1899, the Visible Manifestation of God on Earth, The Lamb of God, Son of the Father, associate of the Holy Ghost, Beloved, immortal, H.J. Prince, died. To say that the faithful were astounded is an understatement—they were devastated. So much so that they became utterly confused, unable to believe that he was actually dead. Nobody knew what to do with the remains. Should they give him a state funeral in Charlinch? Or should they put him away in the garden with the others?

After much anguish and soul searching, Beloved was incarcerated in the front garden of the Agapemone. This was handy for him should he decide to return, which he never did—in spite of frantic excursions into spiritualism and desperate praying and hymn singing by the faithful. He lies in the same part of the garden today, unmarked, neglected.

Donald McCormick in his book, *Temple of Love*, records a death-bed scene between Prince, Pigott and one of the saints. The dying Prince rose up from his bed, set his filming eyes upon the face of Pigott and in a loud, clear voice exclaimed, 'Beloved', and immediately expired. Since this account purports to come from Pigott himself via a certain brother X who recorded it in 1928, McCormick naturally takes it with a dose of salt. But Pigott was certainly in charge of the London flock in 1889 and was probably waiting for Prince to die.

Another account of the succession comes from the then secretary of the Agapemone, Douglas Hamilton. He was a puritanical Scotsman who had come to the Agapemone as a young man. During Prince's dotage, Hamilton had gradually taken over the business affairs of the faithful, acting as a link with the outside world. He lacked the charisma of either Prince or Pigott and tended to be fussy and old-maidish, but he was an able businessman and Prince was obliged to depend on him greatly towards the end of his reign. Hamilton, whilst ready to assume command during the interregnum, was no leader of men. He preferred to act behind the scenes, liked to be the grey eminence of the Agapemone. One must suspect collusion between Pigott and Hamilton, for Hamilton announced that the throne of heavenly grace must go to an outsider and that he himself would issue forth in search of a second saviour of mankind. There was some dissent amongst the faithful at this suggestion; surely the second saviour should come from within the ranks of the faithful few? Supposing Hamilton inadvertently picked a sinner? Hamilton replied that a sign would be made unto him, in God's good time. Thus apparently having quelled any further doubts, Hamilton issued forth in search of the Messiah—he had learned a lot from H.J. Prince.

Hamilton searched far and wide—according to Hamilton. According to Donald McCormick he went straight to Dublin. Pigott, for some reason, had set up a mission in that city, a tin tabernacle, probably a secondary occupation to keep him solvent whilst awaiting for the call to higher things. He certainly abandoned the project with indecent haste after Hamilton arrived with his proposition.

The sign from God that was to announce the second, or strictly speaking, the third coming, is somewhat obscure. The

Hugh Smyth-Pigott, Prince's successor. He was proclaimed Messiah and enthroned at the Ark of the Covenant, Clapton, on 7 September 1902. He was alleged to have enjoyed numerous soul-brides

best Hamilton could do in this respect was to record a certain light in the eyes of the Reverend Smyth-Pigott upon hearing the news that the sisters were in need of a Heavenly Bridegroom. Hamilton explains it as a divine light! Pigott accepted with alacrity, informing Hamilton that his search was over, that he was without doubt the Saviour of Mankind and that he was more than willing to fulfil the sisters' needs. 'Behold he cometh.'

Hamilton's account was obviously for the faithful. What really happened we do not know. A mutual agreement perhaps? It seems likely. Hamilton remained at Pigott's right hand throughout his long reign, both men prospered exceedingly. So in many ways did the Agapemone.

The official revelation, the enthronement of the second Messiah, was not to take place in the remote village of Spaxton but in the church of the Ark of the Covenant at Clapton. Pigott required publicity: the new Messiah was not going to sidle apologetically into the Agapemone, but triumphantly in the full light of public acclaim. The church, which had been completed in 1898, was a large, stately structure of Portland stone. It was lavishly furnished and a monument to the affluence of the faithful which, after forty years of siege, was still considerable. But in 1902 it was not much more than a monument. Services had been desultory and spasmodic, the congregation a mere handful. Pigott changed that overnight.

On Sunday, September 7th, 1902, more than six thousand people attended the enthronement of the Reverend Hugh Smyth-Pigott as the Saviour of Mankind. It was a large crowd by any standard, and not altogether friendly. The son of God was obliged to progress erratically through a storm of hostile umbrellas to reach the church. The actual inauguration service was drowned out by the yells, boos and hisses of the multitude, who did not appear to relish the arrival of a second or third Messiah. Some of the sinners became so forcible in their views that a phalanx of mounted policemen had to be summoned to escort the King of Heaven from the premises. But Pigott had made his point and the headlines; and he knew as well as anyone that bad publicity is very much better than no publicity, and often better than good publicity.

On the advice of the Metropolitan police—who had not enjoyed the ceremony, could not afford the casualty rate and were not inspired by the presence of God in earthly form—Pigott removed himself to Spaxton. The faithful received him with open arms: at least *they* recognised a Messiah when they saw him. He was installed in the throne of heavenly grace where he enjoyed the same power and glory attained by his predecessor and rather more Soul-Brides. Pigott ruled the Agapemone until his death in 1927, and the story of his reign is contained in McCormick's book, *Temple of Love*, already mentioned.

Pigott was a successful and business-like Beloved. He built the Abode of Love into a flourishing concern, renovating the farm, improving the property, reorganising the faithful, stirring them out of their indolence, inspiring them to work for their new heaven.

His sex life provided excellent copy for the Sunday papers and gainful, sometimes frenetic occupation for their reporters. The flagging spirits in the Lamb Inn were entirely revived. He is remembered, not without affection, by many people living in Spaxton, Bridgwater and Cannington today. He appeared, throned in glory, in a tableau at Bridgwater carnival, narrowly avoided being tarred and feathered, and was blessed with a long-suffering, saintly wife who is remembered with great affection for her good works amongst the poor.

The people of Spaxton and Cannington speak well of the

Agapemone. Neither Prince nor Smyth-Pigott did anything but good for the local communities. People are proud to tell you about the Reverend Mr Pigott, proud to be descended from the notable Mr Prince, happy to recall memories of long dead great-aunts who were never mentioned because of their connexions with the Agapemone and knowledge of the Holy Ghost.

The Agapemone was a mysterious, intriguing place, the big house with the high walls. It lasted as a community for over a hundred years. During that time it provided entertainment, considerable benefit and endless material for gossip, to the undoubted profit of the villagers of Spaxton.

Especially would I be present with you in spirit when our beloved brother Mr Pigott, whom the Lord, in his loving kindness towards you, has appointed to be your Pastor and guide, shall read this letter to you.

Brother Prince, Letter to the Bride of the Lamb in London
The Agapemone, May 4, 1889

Epilogue

The Agapemone never really survived the death of Smyth-Pigott. Douglas Hamilton, who took over the running of the establishment after Pigott's death, was no Messiah, and never sought the title. Others did; sons of God emerged from the most unlikely places, declaring their divinity. A rash of would-be Messiahs besieged the Abode of Love hoping to be installed on the throne of Heavenly Grace. Hamilton beat them off; Beloved's Soul-Brides languished loveless, and gradually the Agapemone drifted into respectability.

During his lifetime, Hamilton maintained the strict security practised by his predecessors. The doors in the high wall remained locked, the hand still shot out upon the ringing of a bell, nobody was admitted without an invitation. He was a secret man, but respectable and highly puritanical.

During the 1920s the Agapemone became a private reformatory for recalcitrant young girls. Once more the villagers were intrigued—mainly the local young men who gathered outside the walls to fling amatory notes, wrapped around stones, over the ramparts to the giggling young ladies within. The notes had some effect; one or two of the more daring girls slipped away unnoticed. Not many, however, were daring enough to take the risk, for the consequences of discovery were harsh. There was not only the wrath of Douglas Hamilton to confront the culprit, but the ferocious tongue of sister Eve.

For sister Eve was the progeny of the devil, the same little girl that Dixon had seen playing a solitary game in the garden of the Agapemone. She had passed her life in the Abode of Love, seldom if ever emerging. During that time she had risen to a position of singular authority, second only to Beloved. Even Smyth-Pigott was nervous of her. She became keeper of the Soul-Brides, a stern disciplinarian who delighted in castigating the younger girls. Sister Eve was a formidable woman, and almost all the saints trembled in her shadow. For a child of the devil, she bore a remarkable resemblance to the blessed first Beloved; he may, in the depths of his soul, have been proud of her.

By 1958, when the Agapemone was put up for auction, it had lost much of its mystery. The church had been desecrated, the doors in the high wall flung open. Many of the faithful had dispersed; others had died. The final dispensation never really materialised; they had waited hopefully for over a hundred years, they could not wait for ever. Without Prince and Smyth-Pigott to urge them on, they had lost direction. All that were left were the buildings and its contents. Strangers tramped about the sacred gardens, roamed the great house, plundering the possessions of dead and departed saints. The battle had been lost; the sinners had won.

During their lifetime both Prince and Smyth-Pigott were regarded, for the most part, as monstrous, depraved charlatans. But were they really so monstrous, so depraved? Prince built himself a paradise on earth; Smyth-Pigott expanded it. Perhaps they were charlatans, although Prince must have believed sincerely in his own divinity—he spent enough time and energy justifying it. How much of this was chicanery, how much self-delusion, it is difficult to say. But it worked exceedingly well. Perhaps it *was* miraculous? Perhaps the faithful *were* right?

And why should we sneer at them? Why should we criticise the Agapemone? It was not a harmful institution. Nobody was dragged there against their will. The screams of tortured virgins did not ring out across the pastures of Somerset. H.J. Prince was an innocent; his only crime was

The Lamb Inn, Spaxton, remains under the walls of the Agapemone. In the Abode of Love's heyday the clients of the pub thrived on lurid rumours of the scandalous behaviour of Beloved and his saints to break the rules of Victorian morality. The deflowering of Miss Paterson was admittedly precipitous, and possibly a shock for the girl, but she seems to have come out of it remarkably well!

There is no evidence of brutality in the history of the Agapemone. The faithful could and did come and go as they wished. Presumably more determination was required to go than to enter, but nobody was physically restrained. It was probably no more difficult to escape from the Agapemone than any other enclosed religious establishment.

On the whole Prince and Smyth-Pigott made many people happy. The saints worshipped them as God Almighty and submitted to their will. In return they were provided with considerable comfort, good food, good wine and, above all, were freed from the responsibilities and pressures of the world outside. The saints did not complain. Neither did the villagers of Spaxton, who prospered in many ways. Only the moralists raged against the Abode of Love, lashing themselves into self-righteous indignation.

The building is there today, the great house divided into flats, the church a studio for glove puppets. Most of the saints have vanished, but the remains of Prince and Smyth-Pigott lie in what was once the garden.

Perhaps one dark night customers returning from the Lamb Inn may hear the ghostly cries of Angels and Archangels playing hockey, or the click of billiard balls. They might even catch a glimpse of the sanctified Miss Paterson, weeping over the mortal remains of the Son of God, alias the Reverend Henry James Prince, formerly of No. 5 Widcombe Crescent, in the city of Bath.